START-UP SUTRA

Rohit Prasad likes to think of himself as an academic entrepreneur who combines scholarship along with an entrepreneurial instinct to create a space for policy impact in the telecom sector of the Indian economy.

In order to nurse wounds acquired in the course of pursuing this rather ambitious and far-fetched goal, he vents his energy on various entrepreneurial projects. In the course of his dabblings, he stumbled upon a publisher who liked the coffee at MDI Gurgaon, the business school at which he teaches, and an entrepreneur whose story showed clear signs of having been lifted from a movie. That's how this book happened. Having overcome his writer's block with the writing of *Start-up Sutra*, Rohit is currently working on a book on the concepts and practice of spectrum management.

Start-up Sutra

What the Angels Won't Tell You about Business and Life

ROHIT PRASAD

hachette INDIA

First published in 2013 by Hachette India
(Registered name: Hachette Book Publishing India Pvt. Ltd)
An Hachette UK company
www.hachetteindia.com

SRD

ISBN 978-93-5195-126-1

Hachette Book Publishing India Pvt. Ltd
4th & 5th Floors, Corporate Centre,
Plot No. 94, Sector 44, Gurgaon - 122003, India

Typeset in Adobe Garamond Pro 11/15
by InoSoft Systems, Noida

Printed and bound in India by
Manipal Technologies Limited, Manipal

FSC www.fsc.org
MIX
Paper | Supporting responsible forestry
FSC™ C043100

Foreword

This book is an attempt to tell a gripping story about young people with impossible dreams. To paraphrase a poet: 'What do they know of entrepreneurship who but enterprise know.' And yet how rare are the accounts, especially in India, that bring alive the stories of the people behind the institutions they create. Rarer still are narratives not focussed on super-achievers and not coloured by their sizeable achievements.

When I started on this project I thought I would write

five short mini-biographies of Indian entrepreneurs. The quality of my interaction with Abhishek, Mekhla, and Abhinav, however, entirely changed the tenor of the book. Listening to their stories, told with disarming honesty, was therapeutic for me and perhaps for them as well. I was impelled to go deeper into their histories and contemplate the lessons they taught.

I realized that an entrepreneur is not the product of a moment of inspiration or a sudden epiphany, but a pearl whose consummation begins with its very first breath of life, and is fashioned equally by loss and triumph, deprivation and opportunity, insecurity and self-confidence. I understood that the achievements of entrepreneurs belong as much to the supporting crew of family and friends who may not see the vision of the promised land but share in the labours of getting there, driven only by love. I felt a need to celebrate those who may have shown the same courage and insight as those recognized as successful, but still have not achieved their dream for the simple reason that 'full many a flower is born to blush unseen, and waste its sweetness on the desert air'.

Through the voice of Moojin Chung, a spiritual seeker turned entrepreneur whom I have known for many years and whose life story is also completely off the beaten track, I decided to intersperse the narrative of the protagonists' lives with meditations or sutras on the qualities of an entrepreneur.

This book endeavours to bring alive the truth of the entrepreneurial experience, a truth that I believe has echoes for every human who has ever longed for an engaged and passionate life.

A Conversation Begins

I FIRST MET MOOJIN TWENTY-THREE YEARS AGO through a fellow member of the yoga classes I attend. He was wearing a kurta–pyjama, had a flute slung over his shoulder and carried all his worldly possessions in a jhola the size of a Reliance Fresh carry-bag.

He spent the next five years travelling through the length and breadth of the country, visiting ashrams, tourist destinations, hills, rivers and valleys. I used to say that he had stepped on every square inch of India, although that was not strictly true.

He was of South Korean origin and, with his cryptic utterances of wisdom, broken English, bright smile and meaningful silences, seemed to have stepped out of the frames of *The Karate Kid* to play Mr Miyagi to my awestruck Daniel LaRusso. He even had black belts in a bunch of oriental martial arts!

And now here we were, more than twenty years on, sitting in the bar of a five-star hotel at eleven on a Saturday night, him dressed in a trendy Fabindia kurta and loose trousers, sipping a single malt, while I told him about trying to ignite the spirit of entrepreneurship at the business school where I teach. I told him that students in a business school are typically not entrepreneurial in their mindset, that they have big loans to pay back and placements to get. How could entrepreneurship figure in their scheme of things?

Moojin had turned red by now, which he usually does after the first peg. He said, 'Aaaahh' – a long, extended, guttural sound which meant that he was going to say something beyond his three- or four-word aphorisms (example, 'No hurry, no worry').

And now he will tell me a story, I thought. Sure enough, 'Let me tell you a story,' he said. But the damnedest thing was that despite knowing the song-

and-dance routine, even knowing the stories sometimes, I still found his tales fascinating. And way beyond fascinating when he spun a new yarn.

Which is why for the next three hours I was riveted to my seat, sipping my chamomile tea as he told me the story of three individuals and the company, Eko, that grew around them.

This, shorn of his usual embellishments, is what he said.

Abhishek

THE BIRTH OF AN ENTREPRENEUR

WHEN ABHISHEK SINHA, THE CEO OF 6D, BOARDED a flight from Hyderabad to Delhi in the early hours of 5 April 2003, his thoughts were not on his scheduled business meeting. He had been seeing a girl, Mekhla, for the past several months, and had decided that their relationship needed to get resolved one way or another. He was to meet her for lunch.

Abhishek's morning meeting went beyond schedule. He finally managed to pick up Mekhla one-and-a-half hours after the appointed time. As he walked up to her plush apartment in Gurgaon, the boom town abutting the national capital, he felt guilty about being so late. Luckily, she didn't make an issue about it.

They went to Moti Mahal, one of Delhi's oldest and most famous tandoori restaurants. Abhishek ordered vegetarian and Mekhla followed suit, though she would have loved to have the chicken. The conversation ranged from philosophy to career plans. Abhishek sang praises of a book, *The Greatest Salesman in the World* by Og Mandino.

First published in 1968, the book is a parable set in the time just prior to Christianity. It weaves mythology with spirituality to communicate the message that to be a good salesperson you must believe in yourself and the work you do. After lunch Abhishek and Mekhla looked for the book in the Vasant Vihar shopping complex where Moti Mahal was located. Not finding it there Abhishek suggested they go to Connaught Place to buy it. They found the book and then decided to go to a Barista in Gurgaon for a coffee before Abhishek dropped Mekhla home.

It was a regular afternoon at the cafe. There was a couple engrossed separately in a newspaper and a novel, a man working at a laptop and sipping a latte, and a beat-up guitar standing in a corner. Norah Jones was lazily crooning 'Come Away with Me' on the stereo. Abhishek, however, did not seem to be in his usual frame of mind. He was drumming his fingers on the table, clasping his hands, looking around as if he wanted to escape. The clearly visible copy of *The Greatest Salesman in the World* did not seem to be of much help.

So far, the day had been going beautifully for Mekhla. She had been attracted to this tall, good-looking boy from Bihar since the first time they met in December 2002. Then, he had spoken about nothing but his start-up that made something called mobile apps, which she understood nothing about. But his passion and his naïve enthusiasm did not need any translation for Mekhla. Now, Abhishek cleared his throat and leaned forward. 'I want to tell you something... We can't go ahead with this. I know we seem to gel well, but I don't want to take this forward.'

Mekhla was immediately understanding. 'Okay, but why? Are you in a relationship with someone else? Because, if you are, I'll back off.'

'No, no, I'm not. It's just that things are a bit complicated. You see, I mean, I don't know, but it's just that I am a...diabetic.' Abhishek finally blurted out his medical condition with the gravity of a person declaring to a prospective bride that he was only interested in men.

Mekhla's immediate reaction was that of relief. She had some people in her family who had diabetes and she understood the reality of the condition. She was not prepared to listen to Abhishek's repeated protestations: 'You don't understand,' he said. 'I don't even know if we will be able to have a family together. You should look it up on the internet. Then you will realize what I am saying.'

They parted with the tension unresolved. Mekhla was deeply sad that a day that had gone so well had ended in such an unfortunate, almost bathetic way. At home, she looked up 'diabetes' on the internet. Not because she needed to, but because *he* needed her to. At 2 a.m. that night she messaged him saying that she had looked up everything and if he still wanted to go ahead, her answer would be a 'yes'. Abhishek messaged back immediately, asking if he could call. Five minutes later he proposed to her, and she, overwhelmed with how things were suddenly working out after the bitter disappointment of the afternoon, accepted happily. The CEO and chief sales guy of 6d had made a successful pitch after all.

Why would a young man, twenty-five years old and bold enough to leave a job at Satyam, one of India's top three IT companies, to start a company of his own, be unsure about his acceptance by a girl on account of being diabetic? Why would an executive who thought enough about salesmanship to regard *The World's Greatest Salesman* as one of the most profound books ever written, be so hesitant when it came to matters closest to his heart? Why would he be willing to give it all away rather than look at the medical condition dispassionately and evaluate the prospect of it affecting his marriage realistically? The answers to these questions are not easy to find, but in them lies one of the keys to Abhishek Sinha's personality.

On a winter's day in 1995, the phone in the one-and-a-half bedroom flat of Shri Madan Mohan Prasad Sinha, Abhishek's grandfather, was ringing off the hook. Usually eight to ten people were crammed into the narrow confines of the apartment but on this day there was no one except an aunt who was visiting from abroad. When the ringing refused to stop, she decided to pick up the phone. An excited voice spoke from the other end: 'Madam, calling from DPS R.K. Puram, is this Abhishek Sinha's residence?' And then the bombshell: 'Madam, this Abhishek has failed in physics, chemistry and mathematics in the pre-boards. The school wanted to inform you directly.' That was it. No attempt to find out who the message was being communicated to, no sympathy, no solutions; only a strange glee at being the messenger of news that would make everyone sit up and take notice.

When the family returned from the market and was given the message, Abhishek's world seemed to be crashing around him. Not because he had got marks he had not expected (that had happened umpteen times before), but because the news had been revealed to his aunt, and would therefore, despite the best intentions of all concerned, definitely reach every member of the family spread all over god's good earth. His parents maintained a brave face and told him not to worry, but Abhishek put aside his food that night.

Books had been a source of great difficulty and constant frustration for Abhishek. All the more because his father had been a model student, and because his brood of cousins were all high achievers, sure to use their facility in academics to get some plum government job or other. When he had a good teacher, a teacher who was able to bring a subject to life, he had enjoyed the process of learning. But mostly it had been an uphill struggle, a struggle that he gradually realized he could not win. In an environment where status in the family, standing with friends, and prospects in life, all seemed to be determined by performance in studies, Abhishek became extremely introverted and withdrawn.

The last day of school is etched in Abhishek's memory. 'All my friends were high on a heady cocktail of exhilaration about the future and nostalgia for the past. But the celebrations left me cold. Although I joined some classmates for a hot chocolate fudge at Nirula's, the overriding emotion was one of relief that the ordeal had finally ended.'

Abhishek's father's position in the Indian Administrative Service (IAS), the elite corps of the national bureaucracy, enabled him to get much coveted admissions into the right schools and colleges. But could a boy whose abiding memory of childhood was the moment he had been able to drive a cycle without the help of supports find any consolation in that?

The one thing he got on his own – the job at Tata Steel after graduating in electronics and communications from the Birla Institute of Technology (BIT), Mesra – he did not want. Tata Steel was at one time the marquee brand in the Indian corporate sector. But, as far as Abhishek was concerned, Jamshedpur was the back of beyond, and although he had heard that Tata Steel recruits were groomed like princes, right down to being taught the five most elegant ways of holding a fork, he was not interested. Especially not when it was Y2K, the beginning of the millennium, the year the dot-com boom hit India.

That was the year airports were crammed with laptop-wielding entrepreneurs; everyone and their aunt was registering a dot-com domain name; and eyeballs had overtaken revenue, market share, brand and that really outdated concept, profitability, as the métier of megabucks. That was the year when all you needed to do was add an 'i' or an 'e' behind, before or in between anything to be assured of instant success. IPOs were always about to happen, the stock market was going crazy, and the only people who seemed to have lost it were those who hadn't.

Abhishek Sinha had most definitely lost it that year.

His father had his government-provided free internet connection (an hour in a cyber cafe cost Rs 80), and Abhishek made full use of it to prowl on the internet for eight to ten hours a day. He had never been interested in anything as much before, not even the biology classes, where the pretty young teacher would take them outside to examine the flowers and fruits firsthand. His mother had bought a Colliers encyclopedia for the kids for Rs 16,000, for which she used to pay a monthly instalment of Rs 1200. But now, as the ad said, the entire world (not just a miserable print encyclopedia) was only a free click away.

Pornography was certainly a preoccupation, but only marginally so. The real stuff was all the information about new technologies, start-ups, portals, venture capitalists and the pioneers of the new age who seemed to be transforming the world overnight. Life was suddenly full of possibilities. No more heaviness about being left behind in the race, no misgivings about the inability to compete, no structured lessons; just the willingness to follow your imagination wherever it led you, on a jet airplane provided by the neighbourhood internet service provider.

While waiting to join his job at Tata Steel, Abhishek

stayed for a few days with a cousin, Ritu, and her husband, Shubhojit. Shubhojit was one of Abhishek's heroes because he was an ace at studies, a graduate of IIM Ahmedabad, India's most prestigious business school, and, importantly, clued-up on the internet. They decided to start a dot-com of their own. The name of the dot-com is significant in the story. It was called bhoolnajaana.com, which translates into English as forgetmenot.com.

'The idea for bhoolnajaana embodied the typical portal thought process – put everything in there, and spice it up with a reminder service,' explained Abhishek. 'I used to spend hours on the project. Some others got involved as well – a cousin from Hyderabad, a senior from college, his boss.'

Two or three months into the project, the founding team, now seven-strong, decided to meet in Hyderabad. Most were already working there, one came in from Mumbai on a fortuitous business trip and Abhishek came from Delhi. 'Seeing all of us assembled in a friend's large drawing room, talking nineteen to the dozen about our plans, trading success stories of other start-ups, I thought – It's happening. It's really happening.'

But Abhishek's exhilaration apart, nothing much was actually happening with bhoolnajaana.com. Later, when he tearfully briefed a concerned uncle about it, the uncle realized what had happened: 'Who was the only one without a job? You were. Others were spending only two hours a week on it. Who was the only one spending all his time, every day on the dot-com? You were. Your ownership became so much that you are feeling bad and crying. Others are not feeling bad.' The portal became history, but Abhishek would never forget the thrill, the promise, the adrenaline rush its creation had brought. The experience was to change his life and that of his family forever. The entrepreneurial bug had well and truly bitten him and would make sure Abhishek could never be happy in a regular job.

Certainly not at Tata Steel in Jamshedpur.

'Wake up, you heedless human being!' Abhishek towered over Manish Chandra, who was sleeping at 11 a.m. in his dingy dive in New Delhi after another night of banging his head against the syllabus of the engineering services exam. Manish, a roly-poly, slightly confused-looking boy, had also got into Tata Steel but, unlike Abhishek, was not prepared to give up on his aspiration of being a part of the Indian Engineering Service of the central government.

'There is no way you are going to make it. I know you. Your brain is as good as mine,' Abhishek roared. 'And if we go to Jamshedpur, we will disappear from the map, never to be seen again. Are you prepared to disappear?' asked Abhishek, who, to Manish's discomfort, was showing no signs of disappearing himself.

'Let's go to Bangalore and look for a job in IT. We'll stay with Shailendra and Anantsheel.'

And so it was that Abhishek and Manish wrote to Tata Steel, requesting extended leave citing illness, and took a train to Bangalore, the epicentre of India's IT revolution. After a few months of sleeping in friends' hallways, scrounging money for breakfast, and travelling three apiece on borrowed motorcycles, Abhishek bagged a job in Satyam, thanks to an indulgent relative.

Abhishek was posted to the office in Hyderabad, the city that seemed to be giving Bangalore a run for its money despite a relatively late entry into IT. There was only one problem – his role was that of a programmer, but he could not program to save his life. Ideally he would have liked to get involved in high-level architecture design, having been good with circuits in college, but programmers did not have that luxury. One of the seniors he reported to, thankfully, involved him with workflow designs. Being on the bench for long periods also helped. Finally, he got positioned in the software testing function, where coding was not required. By now he had been rotated through a number of projects and bosses.

Satyam had a client called UPaid, who had installed one of their products in a telecom operator called Hexacom functioning out of Rajasthan. There was an opportunity to go to Jaipur to install and test UPaid's product. While Indian IT professionals typically turn up their noses at any opportunity that does not require a visa to be stamped, Abhishek jumped at the chance to leave Hyderabad, where survival had been a challenge.

Abhishek was accompanied by a colleague called Abhilash Sadanandan. Abhilash had never ventured north of the Godavari, and in his early days in Jaipur was mainly preoccupied with finding a restaurant where he could eat South Indian food. The Dasaprakasa in Jaipur had a delicious 100-rupee thali but that could only be afforded once in a while. Relief came in the form of the Indian Coffee House, where the idlis, although not as good as the ones at home, passed muster by virtue of belonging squarely to the south.

The Satyam team was staying in a guesthouse that reeked of fried onions all day long. Every evening, Abhishek and Abhilash found refuge in the hotel room of Rajiv Thukral, the account manager at UPaid, who had an unlimited expense account and a large heart.

Abhilash knew only a smattering of English and no Hindi at all. But he could program fluently in any language and complained long and loud to Rajiv and Abhishek about the engagement rules that prevented the on-site Satyam team from touching the source code. All maintenance requests had to be sent back to Hyderabad. 'They take three months for a job I could finish in fifteen minutes,' he protested.

This was the opening Abhishek had been looking for. 'If you can program so well,' he said, 'why waste your time here? Let us start something of our own.'

All through his stint at Satyam, Abhishek had never spared an opportunity to solicit his colleagues about starting something. Most had shooed him away: 'You will not only lose your job, but also make us lose ours.' He had, however, found one person willing to talk, a senior software engineer, Harish Bansal. But while Harish enjoyed Abhishek's energy, he was certain that he could not take the plunge: 'I am from Mansa in Punjab,' he declared solemnly. 'I can't understand all this stuff.' But Abhilash was not from Mansa. He was from Kozhikode and was entrepreneurial, technically proficient and raring to start something. Abhishek's pitch fell on fertile soil.

After three months the UPaid and Satyam teams went back to Hyderabad, where the ideation sessions continued. Rishi Tarar, a senior from BIT Mesra, working at Satyam, joined the group. The 2002 FIFA World Cup was coming up. Abhishek, Abhilash, Rajiv and Rishi discussed the possibility of creating an interactive voice response (IVR) application on the mobile phone for getting news and player information. Next, they discussed creating an IVR-based banking application.

In February 2002, Abhishek, Abhilash and Rajiv returned to Jaipur. At this point, Abhishek decided to explore the possibility of getting some work from Shyam Telecom, one of the investors in Hexacom. But he was so apprehensive about news of his entrepreneurial ambition circling back to his bosses in Satyam that he decided to solicit on behalf of a 'batchmate' in the US who was 'thinking of starting a company'. He even created a brochure but found that he was not getting very far by pretending to be someone situated half a world away.

It was time for the Satyam team to get back to Hyderabad. At this point, Abhishek decided to break cover. He told a client manager, Ajay Satyarthi, that he, not a remote friend of his, was planning to start a company along with Abhilash. Would Shyam be willing to provide some work? Abhishek also pleaded with Ajay not to reveal his plans to anyone at Satyam. Ajay was open to the idea. Over the next few months, Abhishek would take leave on one pretext or another and return to Jaipur to push the case further.

'Friends are those who are kind to each other's dreams,' a philosopher once said. And, apparently, it is true that things start happening fast once the intention becomes powerful. While still at Satyam, Abhishek registered a company with the help of a chartered accountant friend of his father. He named the company '6d', after the number of his hostel room in BIT Mesra. A batchmate from Mesra paid the bills for registration. Another friend got a mobile phone connection which he gave Abhishek. Rajiv Thukral introduced Abhishek to a friend at Voxtron, a Belgium-based provider of contact centre software. Through him, 6d was able to access a demo card for SS7, the mobile phone protocol, which ordinarily would have cost a couple of lakhs.

Meanwhile, Abhishek and Abhilash worked till 7 p.m.at Satyam and till 3 a.m. on 6d in Abhishek's one-bedroom apartment in Hyderabad. They had not yet got any assurances from Shyam Telecom and hence needed to explore other possibilities as well. They came up with the idea of location-based services, an application of which was a 'treasure hunt', starting from Qutb Minar, the 800-year-old minaret in Delhi, and ending at the Red Fort, the Mughal bastion that is now the site of India's annual Independence Day celebrations. The treasure hunt was pitched to Airtel, India's leading telecommunications service provider, but in those days before the iPad there was only a passing interest in such apps.

On 4 December 2002, Abhishek put in his papers at Satyam. He advised Abhilash to wait till 6d had got its first contract and then resign. He knew that Abhilash sent home a sizeable amount from his pay packet and wanted to minimize his risk. But Abhilash was as antsy as Abhishek. He resigned on 6 December.

On 7 December, Abhishek, Abhilash and Manish landed up at Abhishek's parents' apartment in Delhi. Abhishek had called his mother the night before. 'Ma, I am arriving in Delhi tomorrow. There will be two–three friends with me. They need to stay with us at home.' The trio was later joined by Saumya Tripathi.

The next few months saw a series of such pleas being routed to Mrs Ameeta Sinha. 'Ma, Abhilash and Saumya have never experienced the Delhi cold. They are having a bad time. They need inners.' Abhishek's mother went shopping in Sarojini Nagar and supplied the much-needed items of apparel. Abhishek's father had just returned from a foreign trip with some windcheaters. These were also pressed into service.

'Ma, Abhilash needs to go to Hyderabad this weekend. By plane.' A plane ticket was duly procured.

'Ma, my friends are now moving out,' Abhishek announced one evening. Before Ameeta could sigh with relief, Abhishek said, 'Can they stay at our flat in Noida?'

The friends moved into the recently vacated Noida flat. No rent was proffered and, given the obviously penurious condition of the tenants, none was asked for till several months later, when 6d's improving fortunes allowed a commercial agreement to be struck.

'Ma, our Bangalore office is functional. You must come and see it. But it is very hot.' Two air-conditioners were sent from Delhi to cool the Bangalore office.

Mr Anil Sinha, Abhishek's father, was never directly petitioned by Abhishek. But he was obviously the resource person behind all the assistance, although at times his wife did not reveal the details to him in order to spare him worry about his older son's prospects. Mr Sinha had himself exhibited a strong independent streak when he left the IAS to start a successful career as a consultant and administrator in the domain of disaster management. Both parents were quite liberal in their approach to their children's careers. But with marriage appearing on the horizon for Abhishek, their patience would probably have run thin were it not for the cheque that Abhishek waved triumphantly in front of them in February 2003.

Talks with Shyam Telecom had been continuing apace. Abhishek found that the first thing an entrepreneur must jettison is the ego. He waited for hours outside the office of Udit Mehrotra, son of the chairman of Shyam, Rajiv Mehrotra, often to be told that Udit had left for the day. Finally, when least expected, Udit casually asked Abhishek if he could build an SMS centre to enable CDMA phones to send SMSs. Till then, the SMS facility was only available on GSM phones. The deal was signed for Rs 40 lakh. Three years after the whimper that was bhoolnajaana.com, Abhishek Sinha and 6d were on their way!

THE *first* SUTRA

I was spellbound by the saga of Abhishek's plunge into entrepreneurship. The waiter came by and Moojin ordered another peg.

I turned to him. 'Moojin, what is the starting point of entrepreneurship?'

Moojin smiled, took a sip and cleared his throat. 'The universe has survived a long time,' he said. 'Billions of years. It has done so because it has hidden its secrets well – one inside another in a never-ending nested sequence.'

I asked what a nested sequence was.

He said, 'What I mean is that everything is interconnected and interwoven, so if you try to tease out one piece of the puzzle you can't.'

That made sense to me. I had been going through various bureaucratic hurdles in setting up an incubator in my business school and understood well the challenges of a nested sequence.

I waited for Moojin to continue. I had learnt that with him nothing is ever answered in a straightforward manner, but if you give him time, the answer emerges, shining with clarity, like the final high note of a classical singer.

Moojin said, 'Because the universe has been around so long, it has an ego. And someone with an ego, whether a human being or life itself, is simply someone or something that thinks they do not need to change.

'An entrepreneur is someone who stands up to the universe, to all that has come before, and says, "I can know your essence, I will change your expression." And not just that, a real entrepreneur does not stop at superficial changes. He or she sets out to change whole foundations, superstructures and everything in between. And, no surprises, the universe does not like that.

'And that is why the first quality of an entrepreneur is courage. It took courage for Abhishek and Abhilash to believe that they could build a software product company when everyone else was focussed on services.'

I paused, assimilating a definition of courage in entrepreneurship that was very new to me. As someone who considered himself a tad timid, I was subconsciously unhappy to find courage on top of the entrepreneur's list of qualities.

'But Abhishek, for all his bravery, seemed to be nervous and unsure when proposing to Mekhla,' I protested.

Moojin laughed. 'Abhishek was in a situation that is known to have tested the stoutest of hearts,' he said. 'But, seriously, courage is not the absence of fear. It is the ability to act in the face of fear, the overcoming of fear, not the annihilation of it.'

'What are the signs of courage?' I asked.

'The ability to give praise to your enemies, the absence of meanness, and moderation in the desire to please others.' Moojin was smiling now, perhaps because he knew I was getting perplexed.

'What do these things have to do with courage?' I asked vehemently. 'These are more about generosity, at least the first two.'

'Ah, you forgot about the nested sequence,' Moojin chuckled. 'It is impossible to describe one quality in the universe without mentioning every other. All descriptions therefore are only elaborate symbolisms, pointing, if they are good, to the emptiness from which all phenomena, all qualities and all happenings spring.'

'Oh,' I said, 'then can we please continue with the story?'

'Sure,' laughed Moojin. 'Let's talk about Abhishek's love interest.'

Mekhla

THE BLOSSOMING OF A LADY

BORN FIFTEEN YEARS AFTER HER PARENTS' MARRIAGE, Mekhla was for them the answer to a prayer, the fruition of penance, and the proof of things unseen.

Her birth coincided with a turnaround in her father's fortunes. He left a job in the slow-moving Indian public sector for a prestigious assignment in the United Nations. M.P. Sinha used to send a large part of his salary back to his parents in Bihar and so Mekhla's early years were marked by financial stringency. Even this eased out at the age of six after Mr Sinha got posted to Kathmandu, the capital of Nepal.

By the dint of single-minded effort, will power and competence, Mr M.P. Sinha forged a successful career despite hailing from a humble background. In all his dealings, at home and at work, he was masterful, decisive, principled and meticulous. His only weakness was his daughter, for whom his emotional side came to the fore.

Mekhla always knew she was an adored child. But she longed to break free from the unstated rules for outings, time with friends, and so on, that governed her life. She longed to escape from the staid, straight-laced Kathmandu of the eighties. She longed to explore the world. But she was to find that, for a girl, freedom did not always come bundled with parental love.

After her school-leaving exams, she got admission in the University of Surrey to study English. But her mother was determined not to let her go abroad. Mrs Sinha feared that a stint across the seas would take Mekhla away forever from her culture, her values and her family. Even though she had a Master's degree, Mrs Sinha's apprehensions about the big, bad West were strongly in place.

On this one point the lady of the house had her way. Mekhla ended up in the cloistered, girls-only Jesus and Mary College in New Delhi. But life has a way of breaking artificial barriers. Important events in the years starting from college would see Mekhla win her freedom, not in Surrey, but in the more prosaic surroundings of Delhi and Gurgaon.

First, her mother suddenly passed away. Mekhla remembers that it happened on the most joyous day of the year, Diwali. On an evening made resplendent with thousands of lamps lit in homes across the city and a firecracker lighting up the night sky every second, Mrs Mani Sinha's life of silent sacrifice for her family came to a close. His wife's passing was a deep blow for Mr Sinha. Though not demonstrative, and seemingly overbearing, he had relied on his wife completely. For months after her death he remained in a stupor, neglecting himself and losing all hope.

Relatives could provide only a limited amount of comfort. The change had to come from within and it did, in the form of a resurgent Mekhla, determined to restore a modicum of normalcy to their lives. Prior to her mother's death, Mekhla had continued to sulk about not being able to go to Surrey. But after her mother's passing she gradually realized that she could neither go to Surrey nor get her beloved mother back. She would have to make the best of her present circumstances.

Mr M.P. Sinha had by this time retired from the UN and started a small HR consulting firm called Global Human Resource Development Corporation (GHRDC). Mekhla urged her father to immerse himself totally in the new company.

'We will leave home together at eight,' she said. 'I'll go to college, and you to work. I'll join you at work after college.'

'You have to live for me,' she told her father. 'You have to live to see me married.' And so Mekhla, through her tenaciousness, brought to pass life's one and only law – that it must endure in the face of all odds.

After her graduation from college, Mekhla did an MBA with a specialization in human resources from a management school in Delhi, after which she was placed at Fidelity Insurance. The desire to see Mekhla married was uppermost in her father's mind. He plunged into the task of finding a suitable match with his characteristic thoroughness, vigour and dedication. Every week, the agency he had contracted delivered a parcel of prospective matches. Mekhla was not opposed to the process but found herself singularly uninspired by the weekly fare that was dished out to her.

In December 2002, she met Abhishek through a family contact, not through the agency. The willowy, doe-eyed Mekhla and the tall, light-eyed Abhishek made a winning pair, and Mr Sinha found his daughter amenable to the idea of marriage for the first time.

He himself was not averse to the idea. The boy's family background was excellent and he was an engineer from BIT Mesra with a previous stint in Satyam. The only wrinkle in the picture was the start-up.

As always, Mr Sinha had a perfect solution. Abhishek would leave his new company and take up a UN job which Mr Sinha would organize for him. Or he would return to Satyam. Just in case Abhishek did not want to leave his entrepreneurial dreams, Mr Sinha also organized a meeting with the CEO of Airtel to explore business. One way or another, though, there had to be some professional stability prior to marriage.

But to Mr Sinha's discomfiture, he found that Abhishek was in no mood to take up a steady job, 6d was showing no signs of stabilizing, and his daughter had stopped looking at the weekly consignment of hopefuls delivered to her doorstep. Mr Sinha's anxiety to see his daughter well settled, his deep attachment to her and the newness of the entrepreneurial phenomenon in India may explain why, one summer day, when all else had failed, he turned to his daughter and uttered the words made immortal in dozens of Hindi movies: 'If you meet this boy once more, you will have nothing to do with our family.'

Mekhla remained unperturbed, calm in the faith that her father would see reason. She continued to meet Abhishek on the trips he used to make to Delhi. She did not feel justified in asking a boy who was so passionately committed to his entrepreneurial dreams to forsake them.

As Mekhla had expected, one fine day in September when the heat of summer had begun to give way to the balmy weather of autumn, Mr Sinha gave his seal of approval on a decision that had already been made. After all the brinkmanship of the past few months, when forced career changes, family banishment and nightly curfews had all been on the table, he articulated only one final request – that his future son-in-law forsake the pleated trousers he seemed to favour and go along with him to the tailor for a more modern cut.

And thus, Abhishek and Mekhla tied the knot in

March 2004 in a glittering ceremony at a glitzy five-star hotel with the who's who of Bihar and Delhi in attendance and the issue of Abhishek's professional prospects still hovering in his father-in-law's mind. The sight of Abhishek's younger brother, Abhinav, at large in the wedding venue wearing a broad grin and a T-shirt emblazoned with 'DON'T JUDGE ME BY MY BROTHER'S DECISIONS', did not help alleviate Mr Sinha's general sense of disquiet.

Abhishek, who used to drive his father's Maruti 800, had borrowed his father-in-law's Zen for a few days. When he came to return the car he was asked to keep it. He had been living in a one-bedroom apartment in Hyderabad for which he paid a rent of Rs 2500. He expected Mekhla and he would move to a slightly larger apartment for a slightly higher rent. Mr Sinha insisted that they stay in a large, well-appointed apartment for which the rent of Rs 11,500 would be borne by him.

All this largesse, proffered with the best intentions, was deeply galling for Abhishek. He had lived his whole life in a joint family and had only one demand from his marriage – that it be built brick by brick by his partner and him with no interference from the larger family.

'Why did he have to give us an air-conditioner?' he demanded of Mekhla, when he returned from a business trip to find his bedroom fitted with a shiny new appliance. 'We were doing fine without one.'

'What was the need to get a new cupboard built?' he asked another time.

The fact that his start-up was hardly generating any income made Abhishek particularly disapproving of his father-in-law's generosity. He had no problem with the fact that most of the expenses of the home were being borne through Mekhla's income from her job at Fidelity. But his father-in-law's gifts seemed to be a message telling him that he needed to get his act together.

Mr M.P. Sinha was perhaps not giving gifts to get any message across to Abhishek. He had no need for such subtle manoeuvres. His concern was so strong that he spoke repeatedly to Mekhla, Abhishek's parents (who by this time were gracefully resigned to the situation) and Abhishek himself.

It was Mekhla who had the bluntest response to all the advice. 'Why don't you see he is not going back to a nine-to-five job?' she asked her father. 'Just stop. Please stop!' Mekhla was caught in the crossfire between the two men in her life who meant the most to her. To cope, she followed a principle that is easier said than practised – she did not communicate the grievances of one party to the other.

Her defence of her husband was not restricted to her father. Among friends, cousins and elders the news was out that Abhishek had married the pretty, only daughter of a rich father and was making merry with a start-up instead of doing a real job.

'Do you believe he can make it?' a cousin asked Mekhla one day when the brood had gathered at a coffee shop. Although months had passed without a single rupee coming in from 6d to aid in the family's finances, Mekhla had shot back without a moment's hesitation, 'Absolutely! Yes! He will certainly make it.'

Today, when asked what drove and sustained her belief in Abhishek, Mekhla pauses for a while and then says slowly, as if the answer has just dawned on her, 'It was love…it had to be love...it must have been.'

There was one problem in this whole situation. In the first two years of marriage, Mekhla hardly had a husband who was present for her to love. What made it more difficult was that they had not had a long courtship and hardly knew each other when they got married. Mekhla did not mind the difficult finances, she could handle the family barbs, but she did want to have time with her spouse.

It is said that women need expressed affection. Abhishek is a person who feels deeply, more deeply than most are capable of. But in his personal equations he is an introvert, rarely expressing his innermost feelings. And riding bareback on the whirlwind of a new start-up did not give him the mental space to connect with his life partner.

He would be away for most of the week, sleeping in his offices at Bangalore or Delhi after meetings ended at two and three in the morning, grabbing meals on the go, flying by the seat of his pants. Making phone calls to find out how Mekhla's day had gone did not fit into the scheme of things.

At first Mekhla would accost him, weeping bitterly and complaining that he did not care for her. Nothing had prepared her for a marriage of this kind. She could not discuss her husband with her father, and did not have friends or family in the city to confide in. Looking back she says the lack of a support system was a blessing. 'If I'd had a sympathetic ear to listen to me, god alone knows what step I would have taken.'

Gradually, she learnt to accept Abhishek for what he was and make the best of the situation. Through a friend she found a Buddhist group whose positive approach to life and practical approach to dissolving everyday problems offered her a way out of the impasse in which she found herself. Aali, Abhishek's sister, and she became good friends over a common interest in baking, and his younger brother Abhinav turned out to be a staunch fan, who swears to this day by 'Bhabhi's banana and chocolate cake.'

Mekhla made efforts to ensure closeness: she surprised Abhishek in Bangalore when he had been away for a month and showed no signs of being able to return, whipped up candlelight dinners when the power was turned off for non-payment of bills, and left cheery notes in Abhishek's pockets, which he would discover, sometimes in the middle of business meetings.

But what really brought Abhishek and Mekhla together were the dogs, a Labrador and a German Shepherd, christened Tara and Laila. Abhishek would call home to ask how they were. He would bring back toys for them, take them for walks and worry about their diet. Mekhla again saw the side of him that had

the moments that count, not the grand dreams. I am more interested in how we connect with each other day-to-day. But today I accept that this may not be the way Abhishek sees things. '

Mekhla says that the process has forced her to discover herself – to break away from her father's shadow, to re-define her expectations of marriage, and to discover resources within herself that would enable her to cope with a husband whose work would always be a rollercoaster ride. Marrying an entrepreneur pushed Mekhla into exploring her individuality as nothing else could have. Not even an undergraduate degree from the University of Surrey.

THE *second* SUTRA

I was enthralled by now. The travails of a winsome girl stuck between a father she thought the world of and a husband whom she loved tugged at my heartstrings with the force of a psychic hailstorm. I reached for my handkerchief.

There was silence for a while punctuated only by the rattle of the bowl of nuts as Moojin scooped up a couple of cashews to chew on. I watched him chew slowly and methodically and as I did, a ball of curiosity rose within my chest, an inexorable, not to be denied, insistent appendage that formed, even without my knowing it, a question that I heard myself ask.

'Moojin, what is the second quality of an entrepreneur?'

Moojin looked annoyed. He never liked that I transferred the entire burden of thinking over to him when I was in his company.

'I feel like I am lugging your brain along with mine,' Moojin had once remarked of the occasions we were together. 'And I do not like what's inside it.'

Moojin does not like the brain in general, not just mine. He believes that the wiles of nature and the seductions of sex are nothing in comparison with the lures of the breathtaking worlds the brain can create to ensnare a human being. But he's like that. I don't take half of what he says seriously. Not that I don't hang on to every word.

But I was determined. About the second quality, I mean. So I waited. When Moojin realized he could not escape, he sighed.

'The greatest miracle of nature is the river,' he declared.

I perked up. I liked rivers and was glad he had not singled out the Ganga, like many do in my part of the world. Why show favouritism over comparable wonders, I always say.

'The river is miraculous because it absorbs every effluent that the human being produces, supports worlds far more populous than the ones on land, feeds beings in heavenly realms with water, and yet never stops its song, never tarries to rest, and moves onward with increasingly stately tread.'

I was getting impatient.

'The second most important quality of an entrepreneur is resilience,' said Moojin hurriedly.

I was singularly unimpressed. I had expected better than this. *You've already covered courage*, I thought. *An economist could accuse you of double counting. Are you getting lazy in your middle age?*

'Resilience is not the same as courage,' said Moojin, answering my thought. I don't like it when he does that.

'Courage is the ability to venture forth and make a dent in the universe. Resilience is the ability to fold up inside and maintain the status quo when pressed upon by the infinite excesses of insistent nature. Abhishek was courageous but Mekhla was resilient. Abhishek gave out a strange and wonderful light and Mekhla shone with an inner glow that did not fade in the face of trials. Abhishek could go out and take on the world because, whether he expressed it or not, he experienced a sense of stability, a mooring, an anchorage in Mekhla and in the home she built for them.

'Resilience is the ability to pay ever-increasing amounts of drama ever-decreasing amounts of attention and focus on moving ahead with day-to-day living as if nothing untoward has happened.'

'What does one do if one is not married?' I asked, thinking about the reference to Mekhla and about all the single wannabes I had encountered.

'Paste a "not-for-sale" sticker on the forehead,' chuckled Moojin, who himself is happily married, although he is at pains to deny the fact.

I waited for a serious answer.

'No, if there is compatibility of aims and ideals, and if it is rightly lived, marriage can be a strong bridge supporting the entrepreneur's onward journey. The spouse can act as breadwinner, co-entrepreneur, CEO of the home front, and emotional anchor – all rolled into one. But as Mekhla and Abhishek's story shows, the marriage of an entrepreneur is not without its challenges.'

I was still not convinced. 'Why does an entrepreneur need both courage and resilience?'

'Because courage is needed to go out and attempt to change the world, and resilience is needed when the world heaps scorn in return. Courage to love the world so much to want to improve it, and resilience when visited by repeated near-death experiences.'

I was sure Moojin had strayed beyond his capabilities. 'Near-death experiences. What can one do when visited by near-death experiences?' I asked, and waited to see him falter.

'When visited by near-death experiences,' responded Moojin without a moment's hesitation, 'it is a good idea to take a nap.'

Abhinav

A COMING OF AGE

AT NOON ON A BUSY DAY IN THE CHROME AND GLASS Oracle office in Hyderabad, a programmer walked into his boss's cubicle.

'Sir,' he said. 'Today is the Satyanarayan puja at home. Can I please be excused for three hours? I'll come back and attend to the work you've given me.'

The boss, who was known to be very religious, was most understanding. 'No problem, Abhinav,' he said. 'I'll hold the fort. You go on.'

Abhinav Sinha walked out of the office, met a vivacious colleague in the parking lot and went off to one of the fancy multiplexes in Hyderabad to watch the top Bollywood flick of 2003, *Koi...Mil Gaya*. Three hours of mindless entertainment later, he returned to his office, looking suitably pious after stopping at a convenient temple to get the all-important red teeka.

Abhishek Sinha's sibling, younger by four years, was a happy-go-lucky young man who had learnt to crack the system. His aims in life were simple. To paraphrase a famous beverage ad of yesteryear, all he wanted was food, friends and rum, preferably Old Monk. Work was just a means to these ends. As the owner of a Maruti Zen, drawing a salary of Rs 30,000 a month, living for free at his indulgent uncle's house, this 21-year-old had the world at his feet.

Before his final board exams Abhinav was not even very good at beating the system. His marks usually landed him squarely in the bottom half of the class. The pre-board exam for Class 12 were the turning point. He failed in maths. It was not the failure in maths that was the problem, but the fact that Abhinav decided not to tell his folks about it. He figured he would be fine in the boards, so why worry them with the news.

But the parent-alert system at DPS, R.K. Puram, was working just as well as it had during Abhishek's time. Sure enough, his parents got to know the true state of affairs. This was not the first time Abhinav had hidden things from his folks. When his marks in the internal exams for Class 10 did not entitle him to get into the science stream, he had kept quiet, confident that his board exams would be good enough (as they did turn out to be) and he would get reshuffled. His parents had got to know then as well (before the board exam results were declared) and when it happened again in Class 12, their faith in Abhinav's ability to confide in them was well and truly shaken.

Abhinav never intended to hurt his parents. It was just that he did not understand why people took such things so seriously. However, when he was caught out the second time, something touched him to the core. For the first time he decided to study. Eschewing even the 1999 Indo–Pak Test series, much hyped for the purported clash between the flashing bat of Sachin Tendulkar and the reverse swing of Wasim Akram, he plunged into a bout of furious slogging that saw him bag 81 per cent in the boards.

Abhinav's determination to do well continued

in BIT Mesra. He knew he was not the greatest of students, so he figured out a system to make the best of what he had. He only had the bandwidth to focus on three of the six subjects in a semester. He chose the three most difficult subjects. His preparation revolved around questions from previous exams. He even spent many hours selecting a pen that would enable him to achieve the right combination of speed and legibility.

When he was with his college gang of 'ten idiots' he was the most wicked and boisterous of the lot. But when he was alone, he poured heart and soul into his performance optimization algorithm. Although he only ended up twenty-seventh in a class of eighty students, he became known as the chap who could figure out the tough stuff and also had the unique distinction of improving his GPA from the beginning to the end of every semester.

This record caught the eye of a recruiter from Oracle, the pioneering database company. Although Oracle only recruited from among the top five students, the recruiter was intrigued enough to call Abhinav for an interview.

When Abhinav walked into the interview room, he saw an overweight, bearded gentleman with his shirt messily tucked into blue jeans, wearing white sneakers and flip-flopping around. 'How would you write code for this?' he was asked, and a piece of paper was pushed toward him. Ten minutes later Abhinav was done. The recruiter took one glance and said, 'Abhinav, I know you can do better. Take another ten minutes.'

'I am good,' Abhinav assured the recruiter (whose name he never found out). Abhinav was quite sure he would not get the job and did not want to waste more time than necessary. 'No, you can do better,' the recruiter insisted. So Abhinav spent another ten minutes and made some improvements, only to have the paper thrust back at him again. And again. After four iterations, the recruiter slipped him another question. This time Abhinav was given thirty minutes. With all hope of dinner gone, Abhinav struggled gamely. The interview reached the two-hour mark. Other interviews had been ten to fifteen minutes long. After accepting the second answer, the recruiter shot a question at Abhinav: 'You are the only one whose GPA has improved every semester. How is that?' Abhinav explained his optimization strategy. He was asked to wait in an adjoining room. By now he was dehydrated and exhausted. A second recruiter walked into the room and asked him another coding question. Another thirty minutes passed.

When the closing bell on the interview was rung after three full hours, Abhinav walked to his room like a punch-drunk boxer. He flung open his door and, without even taking off his tie or shoes, threw himself face down on the bed. He heard the sound of his heavy breathing, felt the tiredness of his body and the relief of having finally ended the process. Suddenly, there was a shout from outside. 'Abhinav has made it, Abhinav has made it!' To this day, Abhinav Sinha does not remember leaving his bed or running through the field to reach the main academic building where the interviews were held. All he remembers is finding himself, in what seemed like an instant, in front of the placement head, asking to see the list of students placed at Oracle. 'You have made it, Abhinav,' the placement head smiled, seeming a bit surprised himself. A roar went out from Abhinav's throat. The 'ten idiots' gang, who had also assembled on hearing the news, broke into an impromptu jig. And then came an insistent chant: 'Shirt off! Shirt off! Shirt off!'

Abhinav had promised a friend that in the unlikely event of his making it to Oracle, he would dance bare-chested in front of the college building. And so it was that he was found atop a hastily rigged table in front of the elegant yellow building of BIT Mesra on a summer night in 2001, stripped to the waist, twirling his shirt around like a cowboy's lasso, doing a ridiculous dance, while an assorted crowd of students, staff, and even some faculty, hooted, whistled and passed lewd comments. Sourav Ganguly, India's cricket captain, had done it in the more august surroundings of the Lord's cricket ground, but in terms of sheer enthusiasm, abandon and delight, Abhinav was a good match.

When Abhinav and his seven co-recruits from assorted mofussil towns in India beheld the gleaming Oracle facility in Hyderabad their jaws dropped: 'This office is rolling out the red carpet for *us*?' they wondered in amazement. Liberalization was still in its infancy in 2003 and Indians did not take such things for granted. But Abhinav did not remain fazed for too long. He immediately invited his best friend Karan over to sample the buffets at Hotel Manohar, where the new recruits had been put up for a fortnight, bought a Maruti Zen and commenced on a round of movies, pubs, weekend trips and parties that was punctuated only by the unavoidable visits to the office. His propensity for optimization was still serving him well. His performance review improved from a B to an A over the first year, thanks to a kind-hearted senior colleague, Devendra Sakale, who spent time teaching him Java programming.

But there's always trouble brewing in paradise. For Abhinav Sinha, it loomed in the form of his friends who had left their jobs to join the start-up called 6d founded by Abhinav's brother, their senior at BIT Mesra. While Abhinav had a great house, a car, structured work, friends, booze and fun, they had decided to plunge into the rollercoaster ride of a start-up with all its chaos, confusion and financial stringency.

'What are you doing, Abhinav? Join us,' they said.

'You are having fun while we rot, Abhinav,' they said.

'You've got to help out. You can't just wash your hands off, Abhinav,' they said.

'It was absolutely the worst reason to make a move,' Abhinav recalls. 'My friends expected me to take the plunge, so I did. The fact that Abhishek was running 6d was not a part of my thought process.'

Thus, driven by emotional pressure rather than any conscious exercise of personal volition, in February 2005, Abhinav Sinha, bon vivant, left a life of plenty in the city of nawabs to join a start-up in busy Bangalore, sans big house, car, salary and sans a solid reason for joining.

BTM Layout is one of Bangalore's upscale residential areas. The bungalows are still there though some have recently been converted into flats. They have attractive colours: pale green, light pink, yellow, even sky blue. Palm trees tower over the street and amaltas and harsringar trees create a riot of colour in early summer. Abhinav moved into a flat occupied by his friends in this neighbourhood. It was great that the colony was pleasant because the one-bedroom-and-hall apartment being occupied by the four brawny engineers was definitely less than congenial. And yet, in the early days, the thrill of being with friends compensated for the lack of space.

The day Abhinav joined 6d, an engineer with

nine years of experience had quit. Abhinav inherited his workload and, having never been trained in programming, found himself totally at sea. To make things worse, salaries were given once in a blue moon, his entire savings were requisitioned by the company for various operational expenses like air tickets and hotel bills, and there was no clarity on when things would get better.

It was perhaps the frustration of it all or a lingering adolescence that caused Abhinav to put the future of 6d at risk within four months of joining. For days he and his colleagues had been struggling to get a piece of code right. The code for the 'preferred roamer' functionality allowed operators to force their subscribers to roam on their network even when their signal was not the strongest in the subscriber's location. The deadline had long since passed and the client, Vodafone, was not happy. The project manager was having a review meeting with the CEO and senior management of 6d, when the programmers were called in.

'Who is responsible for this part of the code?' Abhishek asked.

'I am,' replied Abhinav.

Abhishek did not bother with niceties. 'If you fuck

this project, I will fuck you,' he said tersely, dismissing the programming team.

Abhinav was infuriated with Abhishek's attitude. 'If he wanted to tick me off he could have taken me aside,' he thought. 'Why did he have to shout at me in front of everyone? What was he thinking? Is this what I get for zero salary? If that's the way they want it, I'll show them.' And without another thought Abhinav went to his workstation, pressed Crtl-A and Delete, and erased three months of code from the all-important project.

In the first few seconds after the deed was done Abhinav experienced a peculiar sense of light-headedness and freedom, as if a weight had suddenly been removed from his chest. For some reason, his mind wandered to the time, long ago, when he used to be a very good singer. In music class in Patna, his teacher would end every session by asking him to sing solo for the entire group. 'Let's hear Abhinav sing and leave with happy hearts,' she would say. When he moved to Delhi his mother sent him to a teacher in the Sri Aurobindo School for Performing Arts. By this time Abhinav's voice was beginning to crack and when asked to sing, all that emerged was a croak. 'Come back later,' the teacher had suggested with a slight smile. That was the last time Abhinav had attended a music class.

But not being able to sing with a trained voice, while a serious offence in the music-loving Bihari fraternity, is not as critical as jeopardizing the future of a fledgling start-up by deleting months of work in a fit of pique. Abhinav's reverie shattered like fragile glass. What was he going to do?

He called Devendra Sakale, his old mentor at Oracle. 'Read Chapter 7 from *Oracle Database 10g: A Beginner's Guide*,' Sakale told him. 'You will be able to redo the code fairly quickly.'

Abhinav stayed up all night reading the chapter. He reached office at 6 a.m. the next morning and got to work. Twenty-four hours later, he was still at his workstation. But the hard work paid off. In two days, he recreated the entire code and, best of all, found a way to fix the problem that had been assailing the team. Abhinav was hugely relieved, more so because not a whisper of the escape from the edge of the precipice had reached Abhishek. And so it was that Abhinav Sinha gained some respect in his new company and began to develop a decent level of programming skills. But his skills were about to be put to an even more severe test, and his success in that test would start the process of his unceremonious exit from 6d.

In the autumn of 2005, Abhishek returned from Muscat after selling an 'e-commerce solution' to Navras, a telecom operator. His point of contact, Kim Askjaer, had instantly liked the proposal and seen a great future for it. Abhinav was in Ahmedabad when he got a call from Abhilash, who was the chief technology officer of 6d. 'There is a project in Muscat. Would you be comfortable going for it?' Abhilash asked.

'Sure,' said Abhinav. Oman was a foreign country with the promise of new and untested cuisines. 'Why not? But why did you think of me for this?' Abhinav had not been one of Abhilash's favourite programmers because of his initial struggles with coding and his general chutzpah.

'Because you can speak English,' said Abhilash with a chuckle as he hung up.

IT start-ups in India had a very simple approach to selling: promise whatever you think will clinch the deal and think later about how to build it. Abhishek had faithfully adhered to this golden rule and promised the deployment of the 'e-commerce solution' in fifteen days.

The only problem was that 6d did not have any 'e-commerce solution' to deploy. Further, it did not even clearly understand what the specifications of such a solution might be and whether those specifications would be what the customer had thought it had bought. Into this situation walked Abhinav Sinha, principally known up to that point, and in circles that mattered, for his ability to smuggle rum and coke into assorted movie halls in Hyderabad and Bangalore.

Abhinav was happy to be away from the daily battle of wits with his bosses but realized very quickly that the situation with the client required him to think on his feet, think fast and think smart. He had to elicit the client's requirements without letting on that he was doing so, and without revealing that 6d did not have the solution in question and would have to build it virtually from scratch.

An additional constraint was that the Oman government granted him a visa for just twenty-one days.

Wearing snazzy suits could only take him that far. Within twenty-one days, Abhinav built contacts with key stakeholders across business functions, developed a command over the core processes involved in the client's business and understood the business need for the solution that 6d had sold. Every night he furiously wrote down the requirements of the software. It turned out that the solution involved replacing scratch cards used for recharging pre-paid accounts with an electronic system. Traditionally, telecom pre-paid scratch cards were used to load pre-paid mobile phone accounts. These cards had a pin number covered by a patch that the pre-paid subscriber scratched off after buying the card. The pre-paid account was activated by calling an activation number and entering the PIN. The electronic system, in contrast, uses a wireless device at the retailer's premises that transmits a command to a centralized server controlled by the operator in order to activate the top-up of the subscriber's account.

Twenty-one days was too short a time to work this out. Abhinav's visa ran out. He returned to Bangalore and was replaced by a fresh whippersnapper who managed the client interface while he and three others at Bangalore coded twenty-four hours a day, building the requirements as they emerged. After another twenty-one days, Abhinav switched places with his colleague and returned to Muscat to oversee the process of going live. The launch of the new functionality by Navras was widely covered in the financial press, although 6d did not find a mention.

By this time, Abhinav knew the product like the back of his hand. He had gathered the requirements, done the coding and taken it live. Although he was getting restless and was ready to return to India, the customer was not prepared to see him go. So Abhinav stayed on temporarily, by paying the 10 rials per day penalty for overstaying his visa, until another programmer was recruited to take up full-time responsibilities in Muscat. Abhinav trained the new recruit and returned to Delhi on 31 December, just in time for the New Year bash with Karan and his other friends.

But the Abhinav Sinha who partied that night was not the Abhinav of old. He had tasted blood, he had caught the bug, he had steroids pumping through his veins and he wanted to go all the way.

On a surprisingly chilly morning in Bangalore in January 2006 a meeting was in progress in the only conference room in the 6d office. Abhishek, the CEO;

Abhilash, the co-founder and CTO; and Manish Chandra, famously awakened from sleep many years ago, were present. They were discussing how to sell the Muscat product to Idea Cellular. The door opened and Abhinav walked into the room. 'Why am I not being included in the conversation?' he asked. 'After all, I got the specs, built the product and took it live.'

There was a moment of silence. Abhishek did not as much as move a muscle. Then Abhilash motioned to a seat. 'If he says he knows the product well, let him go and sell it,' he suggested. The meeting went on. Abhishek found himself pleasantly surprised by the confidence and verve with which his younger sibling contributed to the proceedings, and proud of the way Abhinav had asserted himself.

The air-conditioning in Idea's Pune office was not particularly severe. Abhinav's preparation was also more than adequate. His trembling could therefore be ascribed entirely to stage fright. Somehow, he got through the presentation in one piece. He did not know enough about presentations to know whether he had done well or badly. But Manish thought he had seen a chip off the old block. 'He *is* your brother,' he later confirmed to Abhishek, during the debriefing call. Idea informed 6d that they liked what they saw and wanted to visit the 6d office for further exploration.

6d's new product started gaining traction. Abhinav travelled to Malaysia, Bangladesh, Indonesia, Saudi Arabia, and Tunisia to pitch to prospective customers, always returning to Muscat for the live demo. After the project Abhinav had made a special thank-you trip to Muscat armed with a bottle of Kim Askjaer's favourite Courvoisier Cognac. Kim had graciously agreed to conduct product demos for prospects.

By now Abhinav had a core team around him for new releases and client support. By dint of being in the right place at the right time and being successful, he had become the de facto business head of 6d's most successful product. He sent out a mail marked to everyone in 6d informing them that he had to be involved with any development related to the Navras product. Such natural arrogation of authority can probably only occur in the unstructured environment of a start-up.

Since Abhinav's official designation was that of a system analyst, he still did not have the authority to sign off on the deals he was selling. The seniors had to do that. 'I'll do the talking,' he told them. 'You sign the contract when the time comes.' But the seniors accompanied Abhinav to every presentation. Electronic recharge was 6d's best-selling product by far and they wanted to make doubly sure that their golden goose was safe. With only one line of business doing well in the company, there was not much scope for promoting Abhinav. Besides, he was young, only twenty-four, and relatively new in 6d.

But from Abhinav's standpoint, his bosses were just spectators while he led all the presentations and discussions. He wondered why they were not occupying themselves more gainfully elsewhere to open new avenues for growth. He chafed at not being able to take the final step of signing off on the deal himself when all the steps up to that point were being choreographed by him.

While Abhinav was trying to assert himself, his bosses were trying to persuade him to move to other opportunities within the company. Other units needed the kind of dynamism that Abhinav had shown. It also seemed to be one way to ease the obvious discrepancy between Abhinav's role and his designation. But Abhinav was adamant that he would not budge from the electronic recharge product.

By now the halo of the Muscat success was visible for all to see. Abhinav's friends tried to persuade him to help them out with their projects like they had when Abhinav was at Oracle. But the Abhinav of 2006 could not be persuaded to divert his focus. He had found his calling. He believed in his baby, wanted to nurture it without any interference and did not want to be involved with anything else. As he put it: 'You don't disturb me, and I won't disturb you.'

It is not easy to describe the relationship between friends who have been in college together, are working for the same start-up, and living together. The Butch Cassidy and Sundance Kid bond comes close. So does the Jai–Veeru tie of *Sholay*. There is ultimate camaraderie, informality, acceptance and intuitive unity.

Abhinav's desire to focus on his product may have been understood by his peers in a professional environment, but not in the charged, emotional setting of 6d. Nor in the confines of the apartment in which his three friends continued to live, although Abhinav had cordially moved out to 'find a place to stretch my legs'. His friends discussed his growing distance, his refusal to help them out, and his stubbornness. *Abhinav has changed*, they felt. *He is not the friend we once knew.*

While Abhinav could turn a deaf ear to his peers, he could not get around his seniors so easily. 'You are all incompetent,' a frustrated Abhinav had burst out one day at Manish and Abhilash. He used the honorific 'aap', similar to 'vous' in French, like all well-brought-up boys from Bihar, but what he meant was not in doubt. 'You are not doing your work, nor are you giving me a promotion and allowing me to do mine.' Such conversations became more and more frequent. His seniors, already harried with the generally difficult situation in the company, listened impassively, only occasionally shooting off a riposte. But gradually, in the office cafeteria, in airport lounges, in private apartments and hookah bars the word started spreading: 'Abhinav is creating trouble. He does not understand. He is obsessed with his product, not with the company. He doesn't see the big picture.'

Even as Abhinav was finding himself increasingly isolated in the company, Abhishek was ranged against his fellow founders on account of a difference of opinion related to the overtures being made by an investor. Operating from a different city, he had only an inkling of the magnitude of the disaffection being faced by his younger brother. Abhinav, on his part, was completely oblivious of Abhishek's travails. Thus, for most of the latter half of 2006, Abhishek and Abhinav separately began a process of alienation from the company that, for better or worse, had become an integral part of their bloodstream.

THE *third* SUTRA

By now I was on my fifth chamomile tea. Moojin was on his fourth peg. 'Any drive-by shootings in which Abhishek and Abhinav gang up and take out the rest of the team?' I inquired, half in jest.

'No,' replied Moojin thoughtfully. 'Although that *was* the way business used to be done in Bihar.'

I reverted to silence and gazed into the translucent liquid gently lapping in my tall, narrow glass with a tiny sprig of mint floating in it. The liquid moved slower and slower and when it became very still a tiny question emerged in my mind, like a mint leaf bobbing on the surface of my consciousness – tiny but piquant and unforgettable.

'Moojin, what is the third quality of an entrepreneur?'

Moojin looked at me piercingly. 'The word Abhinav means young, new, novel or innovative. Why don't you find new ways of doing things?'

'Because I have to hold my monotonous nine-to-five teaching job to pick up the tab for your booze,' I said brusquely. Over the years I have learnt that even with wise men – in fact, especially with them – one has to give as good as one gets.

Moojin looked hurt. 'I did not mean specifically you. I meant the world at large. The collective pronoun will become necessary when I assume my world mission.'

I had heard that Moojin was planning a global entrepreneurship movement. I had been asking him to desist, mainly because, all griping apart, I enjoyed having him to myself.

'So tell me in a manner that you would use to enlighten your soon-to-be-acquired acolytes. Simple, dumbed-down, true enough to be convincing, not so true as to be disturbing.'

Moojin smiled and his eyes twinkled. My efforts to rile him were falling off like so many broken arrows.

'When an army takes on a dreaded enemy it must travel in the dead of night. In such an operation, it must be able to step forth into the unknown with the greatest confidence. Absolute trust, teamwork and flawless execution are necessary. Abhinav represents the creative action, which alone is able to prise into the vaults of the yet-to-be-born and bring forth its treasures into the common gaze.'

'"Eyes affixed to eternity",' I exulted, quoting a philosopher.

'Not good enough,' retorted Moojin. 'An entrepreneur is not a daft visionary. Inventive problem-solving and systematic action are needed to convert the gossamer of dreams into reality. An electric storm of ideas leading to distributed action produces dilettantes. Stick-to-it-iveness, seeing one thing through at a time, working with goals, are all crucial.

'And that's not even the worst of it. An entrepreneur has to dream up rainbows in the sky, rose-tinted clouds in the morning and claps of thunder accompanying cloudbursts. But to make all this come true, he or she has to bring other people round to his or her vision, listen to their dreams, be prepared to modify or entirely abandon the original picture without easily giving in to the biggest enemy – "the way things have always been done around here".'

'But what's difficult about that?' I asked incredulously.

'Have you ever had a tooth extracted?' Moojin asked.

I recollected my friendly dentist asking me for my choice of music while he put my gums to sleep and got to work, padding the crater in the end with fragrant sticks of clove.

'Yes,' I smiled brightly.

'Now imagine the procedure done without anaesthesia.'

I tried, and cringed at the horror of it.

'That, dear boy, is how it feels to a dreamer, an innovator, a Big Idea generator who has to jettison an idea that has possessed him or her. And yet, no idea, not one, can survive in the cold light of day if it stands proud like an oak. It must be pliant like the reed in the river in order to thrive and make its presence felt. It must be flexible, supple, adaptive, like quicksilver, like a single beam of light streaming into hundreds of tiny rivulets through a grating.

'Getting attached to the specifics of an idea is death

for a start-up. It is wise to focus on the problem that one is setting out to solve rather than on the exact mode of its solution. And since the whole consciousness has no space for anything but the idea that has struck like a bolt of lightning, it takes a special skill to be able to listen to others, learn from them, accommodate the rainbows in their minds.

'Many entrepreneurs are mavericks. They have to be, to try to take on the world with nothing more than an idea and the determination to see it through. Such personality types have notoriously bad interpersonal skills. Their start-ups often break up like rock bands that promise much but implode in a bout of drunken name-calling.

'Entrepreneurship is controlled experimentation. Without leaving anything to chance, the entrepreneur carries out a series of experiments to determine the best way of solving the problem that has captured his or her attention. Having arrived upon the answer, he or she scales up the business with the speed of a bean counter generating opera tickets.'

That's what I liked about Moojin – his metaphors. Note the use of the word 'opera' in the last sentence and how it gives a rather staid expression a subtle but transforming twist. The Paul Smith fashion formula parachuted into everyday conversation, I guess. The sliver of lemon jauntily perched at the edge of a regular daiquiri.

'This combination of creativity in ideation, flexibility in detailing and flawless teamwork in execution is what I call by the rather prosaic name, "creative action". It sounds simple but it's a bridge too far for most.'

'Isn't entrepreneurship all about risk, Moojin?'

'An entrepreneur is not a risk taker,' he answered, delighted, as usual, to shock me. 'Lots of research done by profs like you shows that. An entrepreneur is a person with superior knowledge about something, knowledge that convinces them about the opportunity, when few others think the opportunity exists. There is always a back-up plan. The point of no return is actually only a bend in the road that you can't see but the entrepreneur can, because he or she is ahead of you.

'The first ten employees of a start-up are crucial. The combination of skills they bring, and their ability to work as one egoless whole makes or breaks the fragile dream of the founders.'

'Steve Jobs and Tim Cook!' I said. I was beginning to understand.

'Yes,' said Moojin. 'In the case of 6d, Abhishek and Abhinav Sinha, Mugdha Bhargava, Pooja Kumar, Anupam Varghese, Mansi Kohli… Artists have the luxury of working alone. Even professors can manage it. But entrepreneurs need to engage with others, they need to yoke themselves to the discipline of the business, to slave like worker bees while dreaming like butterflies.'

Moojin was obviously entering an inspired state. I glanced at his scotch and wondered if I should try some myself.

'There are many tipplers,' said Moojin, his eyes twinkling at my slightly woebegone air, 'but only one Mirza Ghalib.'

And then he laughed. A belly laugh that spread to his whole body till it appeared as if the ends of his long hair were sparkling with glee.

I ordered another chamomile tea.

Outmanoeuvred

IF BUSINESS IS SPORT, BIJOY KHANDELWAL IS A BOXER in the middleweight category, with a punch that stings yet light on his feet. He cut his teeth in the telecom industry, building communication networks around the world. In 2003, Bijoy joined IRG Informatics Ltd as its managing director and chief executive officer. IRG Informatics was a software services company that was beginning to target telecom clients. With his characteristic dynamism, Bijoy brought about a phenomenal turnaround in IRG's service portfolio, client base and financial performance. The first two years saw a compounded annual growth of over 80 per cent and a market cap growth of over thirty times. In 2004 he founded a fund called TransAsia Partners and became a 'general partner', one of the investment managers of the millions of dollars contributed by the 'limited partners' who included insurance companies, pension funds, endowments and high net-worth individuals. TransAsia invested in a number of successful start-ups like MovingFusion, Inforack Solutions and Nuvotaz. It was also the first big player to put its weight behind 6d Telecom Solutions.

Bijoy had seen Abhishek present a paper at an entrepreneurship forum organized by The Indus Entrepreneurs (TIE), a non-profit network of entrepreneurs and professionals originally started in Silicon Valley by successful entrepreneurs of Indian origin. Bijoy had instantly liked the passionate, rough-around-the-edges, bold entrepreneur. 'The United States has perfected a system of generating thousands of failures at a rapid rate,' Abhishek had said. 'From this failure-generating machine arise the successful mutants who propel that society forward. But failure is generally looked down upon in India. Close family ties and the lack of role models may have something to do with that. A society that does not learn how to "fail well" can never amount to very much.'

Having built communications networks, Bijoy knew the importance of telecom software and he realized that 6d had an early mover advantage. The fact that they had got some good deals under their belt, including one with Hutch, proved they could deliver. In May 2005, he invested through his fund Rs 2 crore for 20 per cent of the company. Each of the principal shareholders was left with approximately 11 per cent each, except Abhishek, who got an extra 4 per cent thanks to Abhilash's negotiation skills. Some equity also went to early employees and previous investors.

Mekhla remembers the afternoon Abhishek called her with the news about the funding. 'It's come through, Mekhla, it's come through,' he had said, almost delirious with joy. But Mekhla had other things on her mind. ' I was happy for 6d,' she says, 'but my overriding emotion was a sense of relief that I'd be able to pay the electricity bill and have the power back in the house again!'

The 6d deal with Navras, the Muscat telecom operator, had also been signed in 2005. However, despite the TransAsia investment and some successful pitches, cash flow was an issue due to delayed payment cycles. By the end of 2006 the company was again in a situation where paying salaries was proving difficult. The recharge solution sold to Navras was getting traction but other products were not, and long-term prospects, too, appeared uncertain.

In 2006 Bijoy began to look for a controlling stake in a telecom product company that would be a synergistic fit with IRG's services business – 6d appeared to be a natural choice.

Khandelwal broached the idea to the main shareholders – Abhishek, Abhilash, Manish Chandra, Manish Arora and Ravi. Three years into the company, 6d's leadership was beginning to get weary of the constant fight for cash flow. Abhilash was seeing a girl and thinking of getting married. Manish Chandra and Manish Arora were already married. Abhishek had just been blessed with his first baby. Ravi, who was slightly older than the others, was eager to get some stability into his life. Bijoy seemed to have captured the general mood of the group when he said: 'You guys have struggled for so long. It's time for you to settle down, buy a house, a car and get comfortable.'

But one founder was not ready to sell – Abhishek. 'There is no synergy,' he said. 'IRG is a services company and has a completely different DNA from 6d. The services business is about finding out what each customer wants and building software for their specific requirements. It requires technical coding skills but not deep functional knowledge of the industry. The product business, on the other hand, is about defining a software that simultaneously meets the needs of several customers. It is a winner-takes-all business. IRG and 6d are like fast food and fine dining. The question of a merger does not arise.'

Looking back, Abhishek says, 'We did not have any money, my personal bank balance was not more than Rs 100, but I was not prepared to merge with IRG. I did not want to lose my company. I wrote to every venture capitalist in India and the US, but whoever I approached told me the same thing: "You guys have nothing new, you are a me-too company".'

At home, Mekhla was spending increasing amounts of time with their newborn, Sheelvrat. At times Abhishek felt he was losing his wife to his baby. And at work he was confronted with his other baby, 6d, being passed on to his mentor, Bijoy Khandelwal!

~

One of Abhishek's heroes is Mahatma Gandhi. For him, Gandhi's story is all about entrepreneurship. He says, 'Gandhi had a belief in non-violence that most of the world could not relate to. His belief that he could win India's freedom through non-violence defied logic. But he hung in there, he persevered. He did not change his belief an iota. He pushed it to the limit. And although his movement went through unimaginable vicissitudes, Gandhi was clever enough to ensure that it did not die, that it stayed alive for one more day. That, to me, is what entrepreneurship is all about.'

In 2006, in the face of disbelief, outrage, imminent financial ruin and crumbling friendships, Abhishek refused to budge from his position that merging with IRG was wrong for 6d. A stony core of stubborn resistance, perhaps formed over a lifetime of being left out in the cold, emerged to buttress him through the difficult days.

Everything apart, he did not even like the valuation being offered. Unlike the Mahatma, Abhishek is rather enthused by the notion of making billions of dollars. At that time, the Indian telecom industry was adding seven million subscribers a month and was expected to accelerate even further. In the Vodafone–Hutch deal being struck in those days, each subscriber was valued at about $776. Abhishek began to envision the valuation that 6d would command if it had a product with a retail customer interface. The ability to dream of creating a billion-dollar company without a single rupee in his pocket is one of the defining features of Abhishek's personality.

Abhinav, too, did not want to sell. 'I was the boss of a successful product line which was getting good traction in the market. Irrespective of the present cash flow, I could see many deals in the pipeline. I was just reaching the peak of my game. Why would I sell at this stage?'

When Abhinav successfully delivered the Muscat project, Abhishek sat up and took notice of his younger sibling for the first time. The relationship between Abhishek and Abhinav had been one of respect and affection, but not of informal cameraderie. Abhishek was four years older, and had lived away for quite a few years when his father had been transferred to small towns in Bihar. Both Abhishek and Abhinav were far closer to their middle sibling, their sister Aali, than they were to each other. With Aali, Abhinav shared memories of looting mangoes and litchis from the sprawling orchard in their government bungalow in Muzzafarpur. With her he had gone through the pangs of leaving Delhi and joining a Hindi-medium school. He was close to her in age, shared her attitude to life and felt integrally connected to her sorrows and joys. Aali was also Abhishek's closest confidante. For many years, the common attachment that Abhishek and Abhinav shared with Aali may have been their deepest bond with each other. But the two brothers were to discover each other during the end game that was about to be played out at 6d.

By the end of 2006 work had virtually stopped at 6d. All that was being discussed was the proposed deal with IRG. Meetings of the founders were called to discuss valuation. The senior shareholders tried to cajole, persuade, threaten, and implore Abhishek but he was intransigent. The employee shareholders, too, found it more productive to hold meetings when the junior Sinha was not in office.

'These two brothers have their own agenda,' they began to say.

'The brothers have lost touch with reality.'

'Abhishek has become possessive about his start-up and Abhinav about his product.'

People who had stuck together through thick and thin now found themselves unable to look each other in the eye or even speak to each other.

Bijoy Khandelwal watched the unfolding drama and waited for it to settle. When things were not getting resolved internally, he began winning over the shareholders one by one. All except Abhishek and Abhinav. When he had won over the rest he called a meeting where Abhishek was also present. Actually, it was not a meeting but an ambush. A fait accompli was presented to Abhishek. None of the other senior shareholders were on his side. With only 15 per cent in the company he did not have any negotiating power. 'When I invested in this company I looked on you as the lead entrepreneur,' Bijoy told his former protégé. 'Now that you have played your cards so badly, do not expect me not to screw you.'

The writing was on the wall – 6d no longer had room for Abhishek and Abhinav. The terms of exit were that they would sell their shares in 6d to IRG which would later merge with 6d. Both brothers ended up with a sizeable amount of money in their previously vacuous bank accounts, though they cannot be faulted for hardly noticing this triviality in the midst of their heart-wrenching separation from the company they had helped build.

Abhinav Sinha resigned on 26 February 2007, Abhishek a few days later. And after a few weeks, Bijoy Khandelwal informed the directors of 6d that for reasons of business IRG was no longer interested in the deal.

THE *fourth* SUTRA

Looking pensively into the last of the whisky in his glass, Moojin muttered to himself, 'A start-up is a boxing match with no referees. A giant net with wildly flailing bodies, somehow moving forward in the direction of the resultant vector.'

Moojin was being overly dramatic, I thought. Perhaps the whisky was getting to him. 'What do you think of Bijoy Khandelwal, Moojin? Did he do the right thing by Abhishek?'

Moojin smiled. 'Bijoy Khandelwal and his ilk live in a world beyond values.'

I waited.

'Actually, such people play a critical role in the system,' continued Moojin. 'Competition is one of the greatest drivers of human progress, and ruthlessness is the essential ingredient of competition.

'For Khandelwal, the ability to give life to businesses or to pull the plug represents freedom and power. But he does not realize that he is as much a pawn of the system as those whose lives he thinks he controls. The system needs his lack of empathy to survive.'

'What happens if he discovers his values one day?' I asked.

'They'll call him a burnout and put him out to pasture,' Moojin remarked.

I nursed my chamomile tea pensively. Truth be told, I was rather disturbed by the toll that 6d had taken on Abhishek, Mekhla and Abhinav's personal equations. I remembered other instances of friends in the Silicon Valley who had gone through similar stuff. If this was the cost of entrepreneurship, I wanted no part of it.

Moojin saw me brooding. 'Let's go for a walk,' he said.

We trundled along in silence in the sprawling lobby of the hotel. The massive Belgian chandelier proclaimed an electric sunrise while the equally gigantic potted plants nodded in sterilized agreement. Piped music played soothing, syrupy pop. Men in expensive suits, ladies in evening attire and scruffy college students energized by the incandescence forgot their worries for another night of revelry. Courteous members of the hotel staff were the stewards of the artificial dawn, peopled by the flock of the forsaken, temporarily buoyed by five-star euphoria.

Moojin smiled at me. 'I notice you haven't yet loosened one of your well-aimed missiles asking for the next quality of an entrepreneur,' he said.

His statement had the effect of unlocking the surging tide of anger that was building up inside me. 'This is really sad,' I burst out. 'A company in tatters. College friends torn apart. A twenty-nine-year-old CEO ousted from the company he had founded. Betrayal, backstabbing, mutual recriminations. It's not a pretty picture.'

'Yaaaaaaa,' said Moojin. Next to 'Aaaahh' this was his favourite expression.

'But this had to happen,' I continued ignoring the

profound sounds emanating from my companion. 'A start-up stretches everyone to the limit, professionally, intellectually, emotionally, financially. No friendship can survive the stress.'

'Yaaaaaaa,' said Moojin.

'Abhishek was unusual in his desire to hold on to 6d despite his financial straits. Abhilash and Manish's position can be perfectly understood.'

'Certainly,' said Moojin.

'And Abhinav's desire to protect his product was equally inexplicable given he had not received a salary for months.'

'Absolutely. If only each one realized what the other was going through,' said Moojin.

'I am never going to work with friends,' I declared.

'Who do you intend to work with?' Moojin enquired. 'Your enemies?'

'No, with professional colleagues with whom I have purely business relations. And I'll keep my personal and professional life separate.' I was nothing if not resolute.

'Then you might as well join Hartford Insurance,' said Moojin. 'Old. Respectable. Stable. Boring.'

I paused. I realized this was building up to something.

'The answer to the question that lies buried inside you – momentarily displaced from your attention by the perturbation you feel at the present moment – is dispassion. Eko, the company that Abhishek and Abhinav went on to build, could not have been built inside 6d. It was too focussed a niche. Somehow, a separation had to be worked out. Nor was merging with IRG in 6d's interest. Things seem to have worked out rather nicely if you ask me. Abhishek and Abhinav were now free to set up Eko, with some start-up capital to boot, and 6d was IRG-free. Even Bijoy Khandelwal was happy to be out of the deal.'

I was not convinced. 'Did Abhishek and Abhinav see it like that during those days? How could they? And despite things turning out well in your eyes, can they ever forget what happened?'

Moojin laughed. 'Abhinav may sometimes jokingly refer to his "hit list", but Abhishek holds no grudges.'

'So now we'll be asking budding entrepreneurs to first go through a crash course in sainthood?' I inquired.

'Let it come, let it go,' Moojin said, almost to himself.

This was another of his short, pithy slogans. The hitherto mentioned 'No hurry, no worry' was top of the pops but this was not far behind.

'Let it come, let it go,' he repeated.

'You mean like: "Let it go, if it does not come back it was never yours"?'

'No, there's too much emphasis on the possession of things in that line.'

'Then what?' I asked plaintively.

'Every expression of life is a celebration, every movement a dance, every mood a miracle. Why favour pleasure over pain?'

'And how do you propose to celebrate sadness, hurt, anger, disappointment?'

'By watching their movement without shutting them out. In watching, you disconnect. In disconnecting you cease to identify, in ceasing to identify you discover spaces in yourself you never knew existed. In those spaces lies celebration.'

'Celebration of betrayal, mudslinging, recrimination?' I asked.

'Yes. Besides, by disconnecting you also allow the bad stuff to leave, which it always does in the normal course, unless held in place by your own resentment, or anger – or some other emotion emanating from lack of acceptance. And then you celebrate the good times, coming together again, discovering deeper bonds...

Soon you find yourself in a haven of freedom, beyond the pale of all good and bad experiences of life.'

Moojin was at this point leading us back to our own little haven in the hotel's well-stocked watering hole.

'I once threw a rotten apple at the fruit vendor who was trying to pass it off to me,' he said. 'The rogue got it on the stomach, but the next moment we were laughing together.'

'Good friends always get back to each other, to laugh over old times – if they had something real between them in the first place. It took them a little time to get over what they had gone through, but Abhishek, Abhinav, Abhilash and Manish still catch up for a drink every now and then.'

'So the fourth value of entrepreneurship is dispassion aka equanimity aka tranquility aka serenity?' I asked.

Moojin smiled, one of his wide smiles that made the corners of his eyes crinkle up. 'Just let it come, let it go,' he said, stretching himself as he settled back into his seat.

Staying Alive

AFTER EXITING 6D, THE BROTHERS HAD A FAIR NUMBER of options before them. Abhishek got job offers to join as CEO in some early-stage companies. Abhinav had, through the stake sale at 6d, the resources to do an MBA from a foreign university, and also some job offers. They could also focus on building a company around the ideas they had brainstormed while trying to present an alternative to Khandelwal's offer at 6d.

But these matters, important as they were, could

wait. First there were cabinets to be repaired, washing machines to be replaced, mobile phones to be upgraded, laptops to be picked up and microwave ovens to be bought.

As a child, Abhishek had enjoyed his father's lifestyle in the districts. His beloved cycle used to be given exactly the same treatment that his father's swankily fitted Ambassador received. On Sundays it would be raised on a platform and hosed down from all sides by Abhishek, an adoring crowd of security guards, watchmen, drivers and maids in attendance. The flag on his father's car was mirrored by a small pennant on the cycle's handlebars. Abhishek rode everywhere on the cycle although, on occasion, he had to be escorted by the Ambassador to ensure safe passage and return. One day, when he was in a particularly expansive mood, Abhishek had assured his mother who had dressed to go out for an official dinner, 'Ma, today you are looking even more beautiful than my cycle.' When Mr Sinha was transferred to the Secretariat in Patna in a position of greater responsibility, Abhishek had complained to his grandfather, 'Papa has even sent the policeman away.'

After enjoying the trappings of a district collector's

life, the Sinhas had led the modest existence of an upright civil servant's family that, in addition, supported a vast brood of family members and relatives. Abhishek had chafed at the financial constraints. 'I don't want to live in so much squalor,' he would say laughingly at the mention of a possible career in the government.

Despite his aspirations for financial freedom, Abhishek had endured considerable hardships as a fledgling entrepreneur. Hence, it was a happy moment when he and Abhinav could splurge on themselves and also take their long-suffering parents on a holiday to Goa. Not only did the children give a few moments of joy to their parents, Abhishek was able to fulfil a long cherished dream – that of taking his son's nanny with the family for a luxury holiday where she enjoyed the same comforts as the family. 'Each of us stayed in a deluxe room at the Taj Exotica, and so did she,' he says with deep satisfaction. 'Despite all the progress, I do not know if I will ever live in an India where the domestic staff can feel empowered enough to sit at the same table and eat with their employers.'

The brothers also contributed a sizeable amount for charitable purposes. But the expenditure that gave Abhishek most satisfaction was the home theatre system he gifted his father-in-law. As he shook hands with the man he admired for his courage and ability to fight, Abhishek realized that their problems would now be history. Two strong men, firm in their self-belief and their regard for each other would now forge a friendship that would be a pillar in both their lives.

After a few months of watching TV, playing video games and spending time with Sheelvrat, it was time to think seriously about the future. What helped both brothers focus their minds was their faith in the teachings of the Bihar School of Yoga. (In fact, it was at the Bihar School of Yoga that Moojin had met the Sinha family, thanks to Mr Anil Sinha being in a position to help him with the police permissions required for his passport renewals. The Sinha home became a home away from home for Moojin.)

One of the foundational spiritual techniques practised by the Bihar School is called yoga nidra, where one is put into a relaxed state while lying on one's back, while a teacher conducts a guided visualization that transports one's attention from the tiniest parts of one's physical body to the farthest ends of the universe and back again. This process leads to freedom from one's physical being and a feeling of tremendous expansion and calmness. This freedom can be brought to bear on one's everyday experiences, leading to a state of 'being in this world but not of it', an ability to control one's perceptions, emotions and thoughts in the face of everyday events.

It is surely not a coincidence that the ability to disconnect from the pressures of the here and now was intrinsic to the brothers' natures even before they became serious about yoga – Abhishek in his power to dream big without present resources, and Abhinav in his ability to switch off from work and lose himself in a book, or in a new cuisine, even in the midst of the most stressful situations.

The brothers consulted their spiritual mentor, Swami Niranjanananda, a lean ascetic with smiling, fiery eyes. He was intrigued by their idea of banking through the mobile phone, an application of the Navras product the brothers had been brainstorming about, 'My gut says it will work,' he said.

Leaving the audience with the Swami, the brothers looked at each other. 'With Swamiji's gut backing this, what do we have to lose?' They were laughing, but their intentions were dead serious.

From August 2006 Abhishek had begun orchestrating

a furious series of brainstorming sessions at 6d to find a product that would enable the company to raise money at high valuations. With him were Abhinav and a small group of 'heretics', those who did not believe in Bijoy Khandelwal's offer. Banking applications, entertainment apps, and m-commerce solutions were discussed threadbare in sessions that stretched till the morning and ended with a drive down Bangalore's M.G. Road and coffee at Koshy's.

Finally, the team decided that they would morph the solution developed for Navras, the mobile top-up package, into a mobile payments platform. The number of mobile subscribers in India had increased from 35 million at the turn of the millennium to 200 million in 2006, and riding on the mobile wave using an existing area of strength seemed like the obvious thing to do.

Abhishek and Abhinav had spent some time thinking of a name for the product. Neither wanted a difficult-to-understand, technical-sounding name. 'It's got to be short, simple, and catchy, like Apple,' Abhinav said. By then, one Mr Steve Jobs in Cupertino, California, had started the pre-launch publicity for the first-ever iPhone and won a staunch fan in faraway Bangalore in the form of Abhinav. Many names were floated – Flex,

Trans, Flight and Flav – but ultimately the word 'echo' resonated the most with all of them. Next morning, Bala, Abhinav's roommate who was in the advertising industry and had participated in the brainstorming session made the final modification. 'Just spell it Eko,' he said. And so the product was christened Eko. That same name got conflated onto the company the brothers founded.

But there was still some distance to be traversed till there was a solution that could provide a firm foundation for a company. A top-up of a pre-paid mobile phone account involves the conversion of money into minutes. It is equally easy to convert minutes into money. Hence transferring money from one entity to another using the core mobile top-up application is elementary.

But there are problems with using a telecommunications operator for banking. There is no insurance on deposits and no interest either. Ideally, the transaction should start from one pre-existing bank account and end in another. But those who would need a new service for money transfer were likely to be those who did not have access to bank accounts or to a nearby bank.

In fact, in 2006, more than 60 per cent of Indians did

not have bank accounts. Many of those who did have accounts did not use them. Hence, the problem that Eko ended up having to solve first, in order to achieve its starting objective of facilitating money transfers, was to help the unbanked people open bank accounts.

Setting up branches in unbanked areas is generally a complete waste of money for banks. The low number of transactions, their low value and the high cost of operations constitute a triple whammy hard to overcome. There are about 6.3 bank branches for every 100,000 people in India. In terms of geographical accessibility, there are, on an average, less than three branches per 100 square kilometres. In rural India, the numbers are 3.5 branches per 100,000 people and less than one branch per 100 square kilometres of land area! These numbers alone are sufficient to infer that the simple task of accessing the nearest bank branch is often the most severe challenge. How was Eko going to find a solution that had eluded the Reserve Bank of India (RBI) for sixty years?

'Indians do not bank but almost every Indian household has a mobile phone,' Abhishek had reasoned when he and Abhinav had stopped to pick up paan for a party at their parents' place. 'If only one could bank at the neighbourhood paan store using the mobile.'

'Or at kirana (local grocery) outlets,' said Abhinav.

Abhishek stopped the car. 'That's it,' he said. We'll work with kirana outlets. Paan stores are not reliable enough.' They drove on to the party.

And thus was born, one fine evening, the concept of making the kirana store a banking outlet, powered by the mobile phone.

It was only later that the brothers realized that they would need to ensure their plans fell within the regulatory framework of the RBI. Luckily they did. With the objective of ensuring greater financial inclusion and increasing the outreach of the banking sector, the RBI in January 2006 permitted banks to use intermediaries as business facilitators or business correspondents for providing financial and banking services. The business correspondents were allowed to conduct banking business as agents of the banks at places other than the bank premises. 'So that's what we will be,' the brothers had laughed when a friend had told them. 'Business correspondents.'

The uniqueness of the Eko solution was that they could provide banking services in close proximity to the unbanked without any capital expense and with very low operational outgo. But this would not have been possible without the simple mobile-phone based authentication procedure to verify the identity of the customer.

The first solution that comes to mind for authentication is a simple pin number that is unique to a customer. But a unique pin number could be stolen by the operator who transmits it and so does not provide the security needed. Scrambling the pin number at the source and unscrambling it at the destination requires a software application to be installed on the handset. This is an additional cost and impractical in the context of the low-end handsets involved in many of the cases. And so Eko sought to build a process that could be implemented on any mobile phone with a connection from any operator. Such an authentication procedure would in one fell swoop open the entire market of mobile phone owners for their banking services.

In retrospect, the solution, christened OKE (the inversion of EKO), was simplicity itself. Every customer was given a booklet with fifty ten-digit numbers, each of which had their unique four-digit pin embedded in four out of the ten places. The set of four placeholders for the pin number was different in each of the fifty numbers.

The customer would enter a different ten-digit number from the set of fifty each time they had to carry out a transaction. The bank had the same booklet that the customer did, and so would be able to recognize the ten-digit number as proof of the customer's identity. An intermediary could still access the ten-digit number entered by the customer but it would be useless as it could not be used again to carry out a transaction. After fifty transactions the customer would get a new booklet.

This was the final piece of the solution that allowed Eko to provide zero-dollar banking services to the unbanked using a device they already possessed – the mobile phone.

In January 2007, just before leaving 6d, Abhishek and Abhinav had entered the TIE-Canaan Business Plan Competition with the idea for Eko, and won.

Canaan Venture Partners is a venture capital firm that focuses on technology and health care companies in India, US and Israel, and has catalysed the growth of market leaders like bharatmatrimony.com, a marriage portal, and Altheos, a south San

Francisco biopharmaceutical company focussed on the development of promising novel small molecule drugs for the treatment of glaucoma. Alok Mittal, the chairman of Canaan, introduced Abhishek to Sanjay Bhargava, who was trying to float an India-based fund and was looking for a social enterprise like Eko to invest in. He was already an investor and advisor in Fino, another banking solutions provider. Sanjay understood that Eko had a very different technological and operational strategy from Fino. Eko would be mobile-phone based, while Fino used a smart-card device. Eko would operate through kirana stores, and Fino through a network of agents. He also realized that while Eko had great potential, the team needed support from a senior person, knowledgeable in the financial services industry. His fund was not working out and he suggested that instead of investing in Eko, he join as a co-founder and executive chairman.

Abhishek and Abhinav were delighted. Sanjay had been the tenth employee at PayPal, a global e-commerce business facilitating electronic alternatives to paying with cheques and money orders. He was also a former Stanford University Reuters Digital Vision Fellow, and vice president at Citibank.

Manish, their ex-colleague from 6d, had introduced the brothers to Manoranjan Kumar, who was looking for an investor for a company called 'wefixit', through which he wanted to provide services for newly built homes. Arora thought that the cash-rich brothers could invest in wefixit. Abhishek and Abhinav said they were not in a position to invest but were open to Manoranjan joining Eko as a co-founder.

Abhishek, Abhinav and Manoranjan spent a whole day discussing whether Eko should go into mobile banking or into home fittings! At the end of the session it was decided that the group would try mobile banking for a month or two and then reassess the situation. After that session, though, there was no further talk of Eko changing its line of business. Manoranjan, however, did leave after a year to pursue wefixit.

Having formed the founding team, it seemed only appropriate that the company be incorporated. This was duly done in October 2007.

Sanjay Bhargava introduced Eko to a friend in Centurion Bank, which had a network of around 400 branches all over India. Centurion agreed to do a pilot. The official launch date of the new service was 23 February 2008.

The regional manager of Centurion Bank was present at the gaily decorated store in old Dwarka, Delhi, to flag off the proceedings. The young Eko team had made detailed plans for 'crowd control', with posters, megaphones, and re-configurable aisles a la airport check-in counters.

In a quintessential start-up moment, only twenty interested parties showed up instead of the expected thousands. But the show went on and spirits remained high because of the large turnout of bank officials, families and friends. Thankfully, more concrete signs of success were soon forthcoming. Official permission from the RBI to start proceedings came in May, and between May and June Eko opened 2000 bank accounts.

But storm clouds had begun to gather almost from the very day the engagement had begun. The acquisition of Centurion by HDFC, one of India's big four banks with its roots in housing finance, had been internally confirmed the day before the launch, and HDFC had other plans in mind. In June 2008, Eko received a letter from their sponsor bank stating that their services would no longer be required. Abhishek flew to Mumbai to meet the retail banking head, Rahul Bhagat, who told him that HDFC wanted to do something similar with Vodafone and hence was dispensing with Eko.

Abhishek and Abhinav had put close to half a crore from their exit money from 6d into Eko. They were not taking any salary and were paying for airfares separately as well. But by November 2008, Eko had virtually run out of capital. The money had been spent on developing the banking platform, on marketing and acquiring customers. Besides, Centurion had not paid them for any of the transactions they carried out on their behalf. As a result, they were losing money in business operations as well.

But it was the work they had done at Centurion that made the richest man in the world, one Mr Bill Gates, come knocking at their door in November 2008.

For weeks the papers had been abuzz with news of Gates's personal trip to India. Abhishek and Abhinav had also been receiving intimation from the office of the Consultative Group to Assist the Poor (C-GAP) that a senior official would like to visit them in November. C-GAP is an independent policy and research centre dedicated to advancing financial access for the world's poor. It is supported by over thirty development agencies and private foundations and is housed in the World Bank. The brothers did not associate the Gates Foundation head with C-GAP since they did not know the foundation was a big donor to C-GAP. They thought the calls pertained to a proposal for funding they had submitted.

On the evening of 23 November, the day the Chhat festival dedicated to the Mother Goddess is celebrated in Bihar by floating lighted earthen lamps on the Ganga, Abhishek was surprised to receive a call from the office of the Gates Foundation telling him that Mr Gates would be coming to his office at 8 a.m. the next morning.

'I should have suspected something was happening,' Abhishek says in retrospect. 'I had been seeing some burly white men, who were obviously security personnel, scouting the neighbourhood of the Eko office for a few days prior to the call.'

Bill Gates arrived in a convoy befitting a head of state. He was accompanied by officials of the Gates Foundation, his father and his sisters. He listened impassively as Abhishek went through a few slides. After about ten minutes of listening, he seemed to warm up to the idea. He asked a few questions that made it amply clear he had understood the core of the solution and its possibilities. When he spoke, the precision with which he articulated his thoughts and the hidden dimensions to which he drew attention left a deep impression on the Eko team. At the end of it all, they were not sure whether he had liked their model or not, even though he had insisted on seeing an actual kirana outlet. They found out three months later, when their proposal to C-GAP for funding of $280,000 came through.

The year 2008 was truly a time of nerve-racking, portentous and ultimately exhilarating visitations from far-off places for the Sinhas. In June, Abhishek and Mekhla became the proud parents of a delicate baby girl born after a very difficult pregnancy for Mekhla. The little girl, though frail in her initial years, soon made her disposition clear to everyone. 'Before Savita came,' says Abhishek laughing, 'the family did not really have a CEO, although I had tried hard to grab that position. Now the organizational chart is very clear – Savita's the boss!'

Meanwhile, pending the delivery of the C-GAP funding, the bank account was still at rock bottom and there were tough choices to be made. In December

2008, the State Bank of India (SBI), India's largest bank which dates its origins to the early nineteenth century, agreed to do a pilot with Eko. Eko had to decide whether to use their Rs 10 lakh bank balance to pay salaries or to pay the deposit required by SBI. They decided on the deposit.

The contract with SBI was that Eko would get Rs 10 for each account opened, and 0.5 per cent of each deposit and withdrawal. Account openings, deposits and withdrawals were few and far between and low in denomination. The real transaction volume was in remittances.

Urban India is filled with migrants from rural hinterlands. These migrants service the busy metropolises, cleaning the streets, collecting garbage, taking care of the children and serving tea in offices. Their lives are a hazardous, day-to-day battle for survival. And yet they come in train-loads from Uttar Pradesh, Bihar, Orissa, and Bengal. Those who pity their plight may be ignoring the fact that they are doing much better than the cousins they've left behind. Those who pity them may not be aware of the tens of millions of rupees sent back home every month by these same street-hawkers, domestic helpers, rag-pickers and parking attendants.

Eko, though, became aware of this massive remittance operation soon enough. It realized that the present channels of delivery, principally the relative or friend going home, or the money order, could be vastly improved. They targeted this market.

At first they thought that they should set up outlets in the slums and urban villages where the migrants stayed. Then they realized that remittance transactions were more often made in the middle of the day from office locations rather than in the morning or night from the place of residence. They started focussing on setting up outlets in office districts.

All this learning was coming at a huge expense as the contract with SBI resulted in losses for Eko. At 0.5 per cent of the ticket size, and an average of Rs 500 per remittance, Eko was making Rs 2.50 per transaction. This was much lower than the per transaction cost. Sanjay Bhargava advised the team to float convertible debentures, that is, debt instruments that were convertible into equity, and the first round of debentures was subscribed by the uncle of Abhishek who had consoled him about the failure of bhoolnajaana.com almost eight years ago.

In March 2009, the funding of $280,000 arrived

from C-GAP and gave the company a few months' respite. By July 2009, Eko was out of money again. This time, the convertible debentures subscribed by Saurabh, a much-admired older cousin of Abhishek, gave them another lease of life. Between December 2009 and March 2010, C-GAP granted Eko $1.5 million dollars. But by June 2010 Eko was out of money again.

When asked why their burn rate was so high, Abhishek and Abhinav explain that even though they were frugal on salaries, they were trying to ramp up operations and advance their technology platform. Besides, they were making operational losses on their contract with SBI. After just nineteen months of operations, Eko was handling transactions of Rs 100 crore almost every month. The growth in their turnover was because they were directly integrated with the core banking system of SBI which transformed their customer service points, the kirana stores, into internet-enabled virtual tellers. So all the customers queuing up at SBI's congested branches started coming to Eko's outlets instead. But this success translated only into greater and greater losses, since they were making a loss on every individual transaction.

Financial inclusion and domestic remittances are not

even rounding errors on the books of banks like SBI that manage assets worth hundreds of billions of dollars. These initiatives are carried out in compliance with RBI directives but the attention they receive is limited. For this reason Eko was not making much headway in getting other banks to sign up. Nor were they able to get SBI to re-negotiate their contract.

In June 2010, just at the point when the Eko team had decided to shut shop, they got a lead with ICICI bank, India's leading private-sector bank known for its innovative use of information technology to gain a competitive edge. Despite not knowing how they would be able to pay the deposit required by ICICI or fund the operations, Abhishek went ahead with the negotiations. When the time of signing arrived and no heavenly intercession had occurred to miraculously rectify the financial situation, he had to come clean.

'I am sorry, but we will not be able to go forward,' he told Utpal Issar, the retail banking head of ICICI. 'We have no money in the company.'

Eko had gone through tough times before in 2008 and 2009, but this time Abhishek felt they had really come to the end of the road. He could not imagine going back to his family for another round of funding and C-GAP had done what it could. He was up against a wall.

But Eko's angel was not up in the sky or hidden in the sunlight. He was sitting right in front of Abhishek that summer day. Abhishek had explored many options to stay afloat but, given the inexperience of Eko, he did not believe that his customer could be a source of funds. To his utter surprise, Issar said, 'Cash is always a problem in business. I'll give you a credit of Rs 25 lakhs.'

Abhishek is a believer in destiny. His courage in business comes from the conviction that what is to happen will happen. This belief in a strange way frees him from anxiety and emboldens him to take risks. His take on destiny is, 'If I have to die I will die. But if I have to live, nothing can kill me. So why worry. Just keep taking leaps of faith and hoping for the best.' Such a worldview cannot be logically understood. But it has to be appreciated as something that is intrinsic to Abhishek's nature, something that contains within it a kernel of fundamental truth, something that enables him to do what he has done. Today Abhishek looks upon Utpal Issar as an agent of Eko's destiny.

The largesse of Issar was closely followed by a visit

from Timothy Geithner, the treasury secretary of the United States. Geithner, who has famously remarked that the ATM was the only financial innovation of note in the United States in the last thirty years, was excited enough to refer to his visit to the pharmacy serving as Eko's banking outlet as one of the highlights of his trip to India.

But despite heartwarming accolades and feel-good photo-ops, Eko had only 25 lakh rupees in the bank and this, too, would only last for a few months. Then relief came in the form of 4B Capital, the investment arm of a Christian charity group. Early in the negotiation, the two brothers heard about the religious connection and wondered what it might imply for the deal. The meeting in Hyderabad between 4B and Eko took place in the wing of a new-age Protestant church, giving rise to further misgivings.

At midnight of the day before the deal was finalized, Anupam, an employee of Eko, and son of a Christian priest, received a call from his CEO. Abhishek wanted Anupam to check with his father if this group could be trusted. Eko was giving away 30 per cent of the company and a board seat to 4B and needed to keep all angles covered.

'It was late at night and strange things were crossing our minds,' Abhinav confesses. 'A novel clause in the term sheet, mandating conversion to the baptismal faith for the founders, was among them. Frankly, such was my desperation that I would have considered it! '

But Anupam's father, the priest from Kerala, assured the brothers that all would be well. 'If the first ten minutes go off smoothly, don't give this issue another thought,' he told them. And so in December 2010, Eko raised $1 million from 4B. It was the first venture deal for both parties. 4B had promised to invest another $6 million but later backed out.

Through all the ups and downs of Eko's initial years, the team held firm, with complete confidence that the next bank, the next investor, was just round the corner.

'You would not have known our down times from the pace of our activity,' says Mugdha, an early member of the Eko team. 'Abhishek was forever exhorting us to use spare time to scale up our operational capabilities to handle the next big challenge. Abhinav complemented his brother with an eagle eye for the nuts and bolts of process optimization. The mantra of "disrupting on a massive scale" was too strongly stamped into our

DNA to allow us to bother about momentary blips. The frequent dinners at the CEO's home with Mekhla's sumptuous spreads did not hurt morale either!'

THE *fifth* SUTRA

The night had entered the witching hour. The twin streams of wine and liquor still flowed abundantly through the precincts of the bar, but the devotees of the grape had slowed to a trickle. Only the adept maintained their vigil deep into the farthest reaches of the night. Inspired by the hushed silence I ventured, 'Moojin, do angels exist?'

He laughed. 'Of course they do,' he said. 'The angels of our better natures.'

Wise men are like that. Yet again, Moojin had smoothly palmed off a philosophical question without a definite answer. He used to say he did that because my questions came from curiosity rather than a burning desire to know.

I tried again. 'Come on, Moojin, I really want to know. Do angels exist?'

'No,' he shot back. 'None that you can't think up.'

I gave up and ordered a chamomile tea. I preferred its soothing warmth to this mental jujitsu.

By now we had moved to the smoking section and Moojin was steadily chewing on a Cuaba Perfecto, narrow at both ends and bulging in the middle. There was silence for about ten minutes while Moojin nursed his cigar and I my wounded feelings.

'Aaaahh,' said Moojin finally.

I remained unresponsive.

Then Moojin realized he had to break the ice. 'See, everyone is interested in relationships, but no one is interested in The Relationship.'

I pricked up my ears at the mention of relationships. I was definitely interested in both – relationships as well as in The Relationship. But Moojin was off on his scenic route yet again.

'Abhishek's faith in destiny is merely his awareness that we are attended in all our endeavours by a force we cannot comprehend, a power we can scarcely experience, but without which we cannot as much as lift a leaf.'

'If we cannot even lift a leaf without it, how is it that we are unaware of its presence?'

'A fish lives so long in water that it becomes completely oblivious of the fact that it does so,' he said.

I did not know enough about fish to understand the details of their cognitive processes. 'What good is this awareness to an entrepreneur? I mean from a practical point of view.' I was still a bit put off by his earlier retort.

'Life is a dance, danced between this seemingly tiny, insignificant human figure and the large, large spirit that envelops it. A dance in which only the movement of the human figure can be seen.'

I envisaged myself dancing a foxtrot in partnership with a massive air-filled balloon on a wooden floor surrounded by a bunch of onlookers who were utterly flabbergasted by my erratic movements apparently made in complete isolation. I told Moojin about my vision.

He laughed uproariously and spat out a glob of cigar into the ashtray.

'That's exactly how we look to others,' he said. 'Now you know why. But it is not I who says this. Even the science that you hold so dear says that every organism works in tandem with the larger organism of which it is a part – the earth, the solar system, the cosmos. Every cell, every atom is constantly transacting with everything else for it to exist. Like it or not, we are in a relationship with everything.'

'What is the nature of this relationship?'

'There is no standard template. Everyone's relationship is unique. For some it is an inner voice, for others a mother whose goodness transcends the dualities of this word. For some it is a beloved, for others an implacable foe to be overcome. Some read messages in the voices of their children, others in their lifelong tennis coach. All forms are *a priori* valid and the precise expression depends on the nature of the person concerned. Some call this relationship a force in our lives, others call it god. But I don't like those terms. For me, there is a relationship and I must enter willingly into it.

'Abhishek was always looking to hear the inner voice, listen to its direction. He was willing to listen to nothing else – not the suggestions of well-wishers, the guidance of parents, the conclusions of experts, the analysis of partners. He blocked out all of those and waited to hear the inner call.'

'You are referring to the way he stood his ground against Bijoy Khandelwal, the way he pressed on in Eko even when times were bad?' I asked for clarification.

'Yes.'

'But how could he know for sure that he was doing the right thing? The clouds never parted for him revealing instructions written in letters of gold!'

'You're right. They didn't. And so he could never know for sure,' said Moojin. He was beginning to become maddeningly elusive again.

'Then how on earth could he act the way he did, in the face of all opposition?'

'He could act that way because he trusted that if he was attempting to do the right thing, things would work out in the end.'

'So while his gamble paid off, it need not have?' I was not finding the certainty I was hoping for.

'Of course,' said Moojin. 'Many gambles don't. The relationship I speak of need not be a benign one, at least in its outward manifestation. For some it is a horn of plenty, for others it is a thorn in the flesh. For some it opens doors, for others it pulls rugs from under their feet. For some it lays down the law, for others it waits for their verdict. Further, this relationship changes from time to time.

'But whatever it is, one has to learn to enter into The Relationship, to listen to it, to work with it, to use it, to wrestle with it, to surrender to it, and hopefully one day to dance in it in a state of attunement.'

'But many hugely successful entrepreneurs have explicitly denied the existence of any such power or relationship outside of themselves.'

'Success comes not from what you say or what you believe in but from who you are as a being of energy and consciousness, and how deeply aligned you are with the universe. Talk is cheap.'

The conversation was not appealing to my pragmatic side. I needed a how-to booklet, a checklist of some kind. 'So even if this relationship exists, this immanent balloon you speak of, how does one learn to dance in it?' I asked.

'By first accepting the possibility that it just might exist. By being open to a process of experimentation to test whether the little self of our everyday lives is the only mover of our events or if there is something larger. By giving thanks for everything one has, and giving generously from the abundance in our lives.'

'What about you, Moojin? Are you in tune with the cosmos? Are you able to read its signals to engender good fortune in your life?' I hated getting personal but at some point you have to ask the big-vision man to show you what he's got.

'What need have I of good fortune,' said Moojin. 'I myself am good fortune.'

One Fortnight in May

BY 2011 EKO HAD PICKED UP ALL THE AWARDS THERE were to be won by technology start-ups in the social sphere, including the mBillionth Award for the platform with the best mobile content and applications with mass utility and social purpose across South Asia, and the Tech Award, a signature programme of the iconic Tech museum located in Silicon Valley that honours innovators from around the world who are applying technology to benefit humanity. However,

Abhishek and Abhinav realized that without a business case, they were condemned to live forever on a hope and a prayer. From March 2010, they began to apply pressure on SBI to renegotiate their contract. But while Utpal Issar realized that cash flow was a matter of life and death for a start-up, Mr Arnold, the unflappable, systematic lifer at SBI, did not seem to be bothered by Eko's anguished pleas.

'Be patient,' he told them at every meeting, before calling for tea for everyone.

Eko continued to be interesting to investors despite its lack of profitability, like Sequoia Capital, an iconic venture capital firm headquartered in Menlo Park, San Francisco. It has funded a raft of transformational companies like Apple, Google, YouTube, Yahoo and LinkedIn. Sequoia started talks with Eko in March 2011. The partner leading the talks was Mohit Bhatnagar, a highly successful executive from the telecom industry who had helped to scale the business of Bharti Airtel from a few states to the national level. Earlier, Mohit had co-founded Bright Pod, a wireless start-up in the US, by engineering a spin-off from Ericsson Mobile Systems, the world's pre-eminent vendor for telecommunications equipment. Mohit understood the immense value of Eko's zero-dollar banking model, given the large number of unbanked people in the world. He also realized that banks would at some point give Eko a good deal since so much value was being created. He did his due diligence and told Eko that he would like to move forward.

By May 2011, Eko had hit financial rock bottom. 'Mekhla, if the next six months continue like this, I will be burnt out and in hospital,' the normally taciturn Abhishek confided in Mekhla.

On 7 May, about forty retailers showed up at Eko's office in Mandakini Enclave, New Delhi. Their service fees had not been paid for three months. Abhishek was driving to office when he was informed about the arrival of the retailers. 'If we get a slap or two, take it coolly,' Abhishek told Abhinav in the passenger seat.

Abhishek was upfront with the retailers. He told them that the company was short of funds, but that it was in talks with Sequoia and could furnish post-dated checks for 15 June, by which time the deal was expected to come through. The retailers could have been abrasive, violent or, at the very least, annoyed. Instead, in a turn of events that Abhishek ascribes to destiny, they took the news of cash scarcity extremely coolly. In fact, one might even say they seemed to be rather pleased by it, as if knowing that other people also faced such problems gave them strength.

'Businesses are always short of cash,' they remarked in a manner harking back to Utpal Issar of ICICI. 'You generally take a refundable deposit of Rs 2500 from us. Just increase that to a lakh and your problems will be solved.'

Abhishek was momentarily nonplussed by this new development. He was ready to face a few slaps but not an offer of almost half a crore in cash. The retailers, perhaps not realizing how deep and heartfelt Abhishek's expressions of thanks were, left after much pleasant shaking of hands and expressions of support.

The talks with Sequoia were continuing apace. Mohit was still expressing concern about the lack of profitability, which meant he wanted the valuation to be lower, but the general sense was that a deal was going to happen. But it was not. Mohit had started having nagging doubts, and on 9 May, when Abhishek and Abhinav went to his office at the Grand Hotel in Vasant Kunj, they were informed that there were serious issues to be dealt with relating to the future regulatory environment of the mobile banking sector.

On their way back, Abhishek and Abhinav decided between themselves not to tell anyone about the development. Meanwhile, they were informed that the retailers were back in office, this time a seventy-strong group. 'They do not seem to be angry, just curious,' Anand, one of the early employees at Eko, told Abhishek.

The brothers landed up to find the retailers in a pleasant mood, inclined to chat about how things were going. It turned out that before they put in their additional refundable deposits they wanted to have a final dekho of the Eko offices to see if things were in order. They were camped all over the office, sipping cups of tea, offering tips on business strategy and generally dispensing wisdom of the ages.

Abhishek says, 'It seemed utterly bizarre to have them in office again, and that too, in such large numbers. What was even stranger was that they seemed to be on a mere courtesy call, as if they had nothing better to do on a Monday morning.'

Abhishek realized later that their presence had allowed him to take his mind off Sequoia for an hour-and-a-half and given him a valuable breather. There was no time to relax, however, for the next day another investor, Creation Investments, was arriving for a three-day-long due diligence.

Mekhla remembers Abhishek's expression that night when he told her Sequoia had fallen through. 'I did not know much about what was going on,' she says, 'but I understood something really bad had happened. Without another word, I went to my shrine and sent forth prayer after prayer for the well-being of Abhishek's business.'

Ever since March 2010, Abhinav had been making fortnightly visits to the SBI Office at Antop Hill in Mumbai. A meeting had been scheduled for 10 May 2011 at the SBI office, so Abhinav was not present for the first day of the due diligence being done by Creation Investments.

Creation is an investment company that falls into the fast-growing category of social investors. At the time it was talking to Eko, it had already invested in companies in Russia, Albania and Mexico and was looking at initiating a portfolio in India.

On day one, the Eko team was putting up the usual song and dance routine for Creation, praying that the friendly neighbourhood retailers would not decide to drop in for another tête-à-tête in the middle of the confabulations. As expected, the investors soon zeroed in on the fact that the business was not profitable and that new banks seemed unwilling to come on board.

On the second day, Abhinav joined the proceedings bearing good news. His meeting with SBI in Mumbai had gone well.

When he had entered Mr Arnold's office, Mr Arnold was eating a savoury mixture. 'Have some,' he suggested. 'And let's drink a cup of tea.'

'Sir,' Abhinav said. 'How are you?'

'Fine, fine,' said Mr Arnold. 'Yes, my novel is coming along well.' He had been writing a voluminous historical novel set in ancient India and Abhinav had some of its choicest extracts.

'Oh,' Mr Arnold then said. 'I have something for you.' He reached into his drawer and took out a few pages. Abhinav cringed at the thought of having to go through the latest updates in *Ashokan Dilemmas*. But he was pleasantly surprised. 'This is the new agreement. See if it is okay,' said Mr Arnold.

Abhinav was handed two pieces of paper. He raced through the opening paragraphs of the usual drivel that agreements are wont to have and arrived at the parts that mattered. When he saw the figure, he did not register it immediately for fear he might have been mistaken. He looked again and the number stayed the same. Fifty rupees. Fifty rupees per remittance. Twenty for the retailer and thirty to Eko. *Eko's share had increased from Rs 2.50 to Rs 30 in one stroke, a twelve-fold increase.*

'I'll sign on this right away, sir. Right away,' said Abhinav.

'No, no, you take it back to your office, go over it carefully and send me an email accepting the terms,' said Mr Arnold, beaming at Abhinav. 'And great, here comes the tea.'

When Abhishek got the news his first response was to call up Mohit Bhatnagar at Sequoia to ask if they were still interested. Mohit said that he would like to see how things worked for a month before committing. But Eko did not have the luxury of waiting for Sequoia and went ahead with their negotiations with Creation.

Today Abhishek Sinha, who had been outsmarted by Bijoy Khandelwal at 6d, rues the fact that he did not use one final negotiating ploy with Sequoia. 'I should have told Mohit that we were talking to Creation,' he says.

The second day of due diligence began with a reprise of the profitability challenge. Abhinav and the Eko team heard Creation out for some time. Then Abhinav got up and handed the visitors copies of the latest agreement.

Patrick Fisher, the founder and CEO of Creation Investments, was leading the team. Patrick is an extremely energetic, achievement-oriented, enthusiastic finance professional with his heart in the right place. He was first delighted and then openly incredulous, a natural reaction from anyone faced with this instantaneous and almost outlandish reversal in a company's fortunes in the middle of a due diligence. Besides, Patrick is from Chicago – he cannot just be told, he has to be shown!

That Creation would make the investment if the new contract was authentic was a foregone conclusion. The process to check the veracity of the Eko claim was nothing if not thorough. Abhinav's laptop was requisitioned to scour through all the correspondence with SBI, an expert flown in from the US to check the authenticity of email communications, and a meeting was requested with SBI in which Eko was to merely listen-in.

Abhishek and Abhinav arrived at the SBI office in Mumbai for the conference call with Creation. Mr Arnold was briefed on the important points he must touch upon. Then, with all tasks completed, the two brothers went to the nearby beach and watched the sea crash against the wall as they waited for news of the conference to come in.

After 45 minutes Abhinav's phone rang. 'I told them everything,' said Mr Arnold cheerfully. 'I think they were very happy.'

Next, the Eko team was given a long list of documents that needed to be furnished before the transaction could come through.

'Company incorporation certificate, articles of association, income tax returns since inception, financial statements since inception, term sheet, customer contracts, RBI permissions, share certificates, no-liability declarations…' Abhishek groaned. He had never liked paperwork, but between him and freedom for his company stood a mountain of documentation. To make things worse, Abhinav was leaving that night for the US for some previously lined-up meetings with investors. Given their experiences in the past, the brothers were not willing to regard the deal as done till the money hit the bank.

Abhishek called the office of GHRDC, Mekhla's father's company where Mekhla now worked part-time.

'Mekhla, you've got to come over for a day or two to anchor this,' he pleaded. Mekhla freed herself from work and came right over.

Abhinav had to sign all the papers before he left for the US. Mekhla suggested that he sign a number of blank sheets as well just in case some other papers needed to be prepared.

The entire office had become a document warehouse. The chartered accountant and lawyer were in attendance. The photocopy machine was working full-time on this deadline alone. At 10 p.m. Abhishek stepped out to drop Abhinav to the airport. Abhinav was not happy that he had to leave in the middle of all the work but Abhishek assured him that he had done everything he needed to. After dropping Abhinav, Abhishek returned to office.

Abhinav checked in his baggage and went through immigration. He settled into a chair with a book, when suddenly his phone rang. It was Abhishek. 'Abhinav, we need one more signature from you. Can you please come back?' It was midnight. Abhinav's plane was due to leave at 2 a.m.

'I've crossed immigration, I don't think I can turn back,' said Abhinav.

'Are you sure? Okay, I'll check if Papa can help,' said Abhishek.

Abhishek's father called a senior customs official and explained the predicament. The customs official called up the officer on duty at Delhi Airport and asked him to allow Abhinav to exit.

By now there was only an hour left for the flight. 'Should I take a cab back to office?' Abhinav asked.

'No, you might miss your flight. We'll come,' said Abhishek.

Abhishek and Mekhla dashed to the airport and met Abhinav at the entrance. The signature was taken and Abhinav was the last person to board his flight. He switched off his cell phone and fell into a deep sleep.

The next morning when he switched on his cell phone he saw a three-word message from Abhishek: 'Money in account.' Without waiting for the last required document, at 2.15 a.m. the previous night, just as Abhinav's plane was taxiing for takeoff, Patrick Fisher had wired the money. From start to finish, the deal had taken fifteen days.

Moojin is sitting in Abhishek and Mekhla's roomy Gurgaon apartment while their five-year-old son Sheelvrat plays with the latest kiddie craze, the wheelies, and their three-year-old daughter, Savita, tries to climb onto her father's back. 'I missed most of the first five years of my son's life and the first three years of my daughter's,' says Abhishek remorsefully, as his daughter romps all over him. 'Come to think of it, Mekhla and I never did the stuff that young couples do – going to the disco, watching movies, or making those weekend trips with friends.'

'We did not even have a honeymoon,' says Mekhla, laughing.

Abhishek looks genuinely guilty. There is silence for a few moments.

Then, shutting everything else out, oblivious of Moojin's presence, Abhishek starts planning a family vacation to the backwaters of Kerala. Moojin tiptoes out, leaving a family intent on making up for lost time.

Moojin

A FEATHER DANCING UPON THE BREEZE

IT WAS NOW THREE IN THE MORNING. THE TROUPE of Saturday night revellers was slowly thinning out. I had been up since 6 a.m. the previous morning and was utterly exhausted, yet totally absorbed in the story I had just heard. And despite all that I had to reflect on, I was not done. I still did not have the final piece of the jigsaw.

For years the man before me had promised intriguing possibilities in my life. But over twenty years had passed and those possibilities seemed to be disappearing into thin air. I myself was not the bright-eyed, foolish-but-endearing kid he had first met. In fact, I probably had as much grey hair as Moojin. I needed to know if he really had the goods.

'Moojin, after the five years you spent travelling around India, you went back to Korea. We hardly had any news of you for the next fifteen years, till you recently returned. Tell me your story. What did your spiritual quest teach you? How have you chosen to live your life?'

'Aaaahh.'

And then with the same lack of fuss with which he narrated the tale of Eko, Moojin told me his story. This, shorn of embellishments, is what he said.

He was born in Changsoo, a small village surrounded by mountains in the south-western part of Korea. He was christened Chang-Kwon at birth (Moojin was a *nom de plume* he adopted later) and was the son of Jae-Keun Chung and Sook-Ja Jang. At birth he had a deep cleft in his palate. The surgical operation to rectify his condition was long and arduous and cost his middle-class family a lot of money. The results of the surgery were not as expected and young Moojin continued to have trouble forming words. Four other children, all healthy and happy, were born to the Chungs. Moojin was regarded as the unlucky one by his grandmother.

The remaining scars of the cleft palate made young Moojin a target of merciless ribbing by his school friends. The family had by now moved to the biggest city in their province, Jeonju, and the parents were struggling to establish themselves in their new world. They did not realize the trauma their eldest son was going through.

Moojin became silent and brooding. He kept to himself and was prone to bursts of rage. He had only one friend in school, a waif-like lad called Noh, who did not seem to notice his scar. Noh and he were soon inseparable and such was their sense of union that they would exchange the name tags they used to wear. But Noh moved away to a different school in the sixth grade and Moojin was once again left to his own devices.

As a child, Moojin had a weak constitution, but one remarkable physical quality – stamina and endurance to bear the pain of intense training. He joined tae kwon do classes, a common feature of Seoul's middle-class neighbourhood parks, and soon became a proficient practitioner.

But the ribbing did not stop till Moojin actually took recourse to his fighting skills. On many days he would return home with a black-eye earned while taking on a gang of bullies. Gradually people realized they could not mess with this tough young man.

Like Abhishek, Moojin did not have a yen for studies. In college, at a time when the democracy of South Korea was being challenged by the military establishment, he distinguished himself by joining a group of students who, like their contemporaries, the hippies in the West, were dedicated to pacifism and natural living. In his second year of college, Moojin dropped out and started living alone in the hills around Seoul. Later he moved to Jiri Mountain, considered holy by many Koreans. After three years of solitude he started an institute to teach Hatha Yoga. He also formed a community of people interested in learning and practising traditional Korean musical instruments. The community got a good response from the young Koreans. He was also fond of bikes, and although he could never afford a large bike he had the pick of Harleys and Kawasakis due to his growing band of admirers.

Among the group of friends that had gathered around Moojin was a vivacious, good-natured girl called Chun Hee. Chun Hee was one of the prime movers of the group and she brought in a number of friends to join. She was taken up by Moojin's idealism, his naiveté, and his curious blend of vulnerability and toughness. She called him 'the Korean dreamer,' in juxtaposition to 'the American dreamer', Martin Luther King.

Moojin found himself increasingly drawn to Chun Hee. But he realized that while she held him in the highest regard and affection, she could not think of him romantically. He did not ask, and she did not say, but the message was clear to both of them. After a few years the community broke up but Moojin continued teaching yoga to a small group of faithful followers and organizing events of traditional Korean music and dance.

While Moojin was hailed as a new age Thoreau and Martin Luther King by his friends, his dreams did not lie in the US but in India. And yet it was the US that was his first stop when he left South Korea. In the middle of the 1980s his mother passed away after being afflicted with cancer and the family decided to follow an older sister to the US. They first spent two years in Dallas and then took up residence in a small house with a garden in Fort Lee, a suburb of New Jersey. The Chung family started running a departmental store.

Moojin was working at a regular job for the first time in his life. Life under the Reagan–Bush administrations was tough for small businesses. To make things worse, there was a long-running feud between the Korean community and the African-Americans. Running a store exposed Moojin to the seamy underbelly of the US.

He missed Korea terribly. With very poor skills in English, a visceral dislike of the utilitarian American way of life he saw around him, and a work environment that brought his street-fighting instincts to the fore, he was miserable. The evenings spent listening to his vast music collection with a group of friends and a bottle of scotch were his only refuge. He grew his hair long and swayed as Marley exhorted the 'buffalo soldier' to stand up, or consoled the man aching for love with 'No Woman No Cry'.

Ever since his childhood Moojin had experienced sharp and frequent mood swings. One moment he would be overjoyed, full of energy and brimful with love for the world. The next moment he would be depressed and resentful of everyone. He had found solace with the monks of Zen Buddhism when he had lived in the mountains in Korea. He also loved leafing through his copy of the Bhagavad Gita.

One day, he came across a book called *Autobiography of a Yogi* by Paramhansa Yogananda. He read the book in one sitting of eight hours, re-read it to underline important portions and then went back a few more times to experience again the magic he had felt.

The book is the autobiography of one of the pioneers of the worldwide yoga movement, Paramhansa Yogananda, and the remarkable men and women he came in contact with in his years of travelling across the globe. In describing his encounters with the yogis, Paramahansa also elucidates the philosophies, beliefs and practices that underpin their way of life. When reading the book, the desire to visit the ashrams mentioned in the book and meet the new generation of wise men in India grew in Moojin's mind with redoubled vigour.

Although he was the oldest of the siblings and expected to take responsibility for the family, Moojin felt he had done enough. He had worked twelve hours a day for four years to stabilize the grocery store. He felt he had earned the right to follow the burning desires of his heart.

So, one day, emboldened by the credit card given to him by his brothers, he took a plane to India. Shortly thereafter, we met in Delhi. It was the winter of 1989.

In India, Moojin first gravitated toward the ashram of a guru who taught an advanced technique of Pranayama to his disciples. The head of the monastery, a graceful American monk, took kindly to the intense, obviously sincere South Korean. Moojin spent months meditating for up to ten hours a day in the monastery.

During his time there, he visited other pilgrimage and tourist spots – Bodh Gaya, Elephanta, Kerala, Ajmer, Dharamshala. He was welcomed with open arms in every monastery he went to and was offered automatic entries into their monastic orders. But Moojin wanted only to be a wandering sadhu, a feather floating upon the breeze in India, experiencing his own being in different ways suggested by various paths. Gradually he stopped returning to the ashram that had been his anchor in his first year in India and wandered around, unfettered, for almost five years.

In this time, Moojin underwent various transformative experiences – a spontaneous six months of complete silence at Manali and Dharamshala; an hours-long epiphany at Mathura where, like the sages of old, he did not know where his personality ended and the world began; three days and nights of being lost in meditation in a cave in the Thar Desert; a period of almost crazed exhilaration at an ashram in Kollam, Kerala.

Wherever he went, he would buy armfuls of books and ship them back to my house to be stored till he returned home. He would also write letters to me from his various far-flung locations. 'Dear Blessed Soul Rohit-ji,' he wrote from one of his outposts, 'by the grace of whatever, two days ago, sitting in my hotel room, I found myself possessed of the settled conviction that I was spread all over the room and that even the table was part of my own self. This kind of feeling I experience all the time now, though with differing degrees of intensity. Quite strange.' His style of correspondence too evolved over the years. In the beginning, he would address me with the respectful suffix of 'ji' but, over time, Moojin became much more informal. These days he usually initiates communication with a crisp 'Haanji', which is his Indian version of 'Yo man.'

And I would always be presented with pearls of his wisdom and insight. Once, I was standing at a railway station with Moojin when he told me that for a person of sensitivity even a train could arouse a sense of fear.

'Even a stationary, inert, perfectly well-meaning train showing absolutely no signs of hurling itself at you like a snorting bull?' I asked, wanting to check if I had heard correctly.

'Yes,' he replied gravely, pointing at an innocuous enough freight wagon in front of us, 'even that train there.'

Now, as I write this, I feel that he may have meant awe instead of fear. But then, with Moojin, who's to know?

Another time, we were sitting at the India Coffee House, an old hangout of artists, poets and intellectuals in Connaught Place, when Moojin remarked, 'I don't know if it is possible to maintain awareness of one's self all the time, but in any case I'm not there yet. It may take another twenty years...who cares.'

'I have no more hope left,' I also remember him saying. 'I have nothing more to do.' By this he perhaps meant that the dawns of fleeting joy that beset the lives of ordinary men and women were a thing of the past for him. He had found a more robust anchorage.

In the middle of Moojin's first sojourn through India I left for graduate studies in the US, where I enjoyed the hospitality of his silent but warm and loving family. On weekends I would escape from the drudgery of household chores in my shared apartment to Moojin's home in Fort Lee, New Jersey, where I would sleep late, eat lots of great Korean food and occasionally go out for a beer and sushi with Moojin's brothers, Joon Hong and Yoo Jung.

I was always allotted Moojin's room on the top floor of the house when I stayed there. It was really an attic, but it had atmosphere. All the furniture was floor-level, wood with off-white and beige fabric. There was a large, low-hanging spherical paper lamp with a Zen painting on it and the walls were stacked with books and music. Moojin certainly had an eclectic taste – everything, from Leonard Cohen to traditional Korean music, from Plato's *Republic* to Ram Dass's *Be Here Now*, found a space in the niches of his cavernous library.

Waking up late on weekend mornings, I would absorb the smells of the simple Korean home wafting up from the kitchen – rice in the cooker, soybean paste soup called Toenjan on the stove, and bottles of kimchi stacked in the kitchen cabinets. And I would imagine Moojin waking up in this room dreaming of an unfettered life, dreaming of meetings with savants, dreaming of a land called India.

One day, as I read his well-thumbed copy of *The Autobiography of a Yogi*, the book that had so inflamed his imagination, a black-and-white photograph of a strikingly beautiful long-haired young man fell out. He was seated, rapt in inner contemplation and holding in one raised hand the drum of Shiva, the damru, its two dancing threads coiled like snakes, about to be released to strike the skins, as if to set a universal rhythm into motion. And I thought then of how Moojin had told me that in Goa one evening, with the sun sinking in the distant horizon like a Spanish galleon and the sounds of 'Hotel California' streaming out of a seafront shack, he had started dancing, with his ponytail swinging this way and that, unmindful of the gaggle of tourists and locals – a South Korean sadhu, grooving to a rock-and-roll standard, unshackled from his American existence, at home in the land of his dreams, free at last.

Moojin did not know it at the time, but his days of gypsy wanderings were drawing to a close.

In a letter written many years later, Moojin confided:

At a certain period, at a certain place, I understood from the bottom of my being that there couldn't be anyone in this world who knew me better than myself. From then on, wandering, seeking and meeting ceased to have any meaning for me.

Unlike before, I had no place to go, no people to meet, no things to do…hence I settled myself in a remote hamlet near Manali in winter. Nearly half a year passed in complete silence with heavenly peace. This spontaneous silence was broken when I shifted to Dharamshala to avoid the crowd of tourists at Manali and encountered some Korean people whom I had known since the '80s.

That encounter not only broke my silence, it also marked the beginning of the end of my reclusive, free lifestyle. At my friends' insistence, I made up my mind to write a guide book on India for Korean tourists.

The reason I decided to write a guide book on India for Koreans, despite knowing it would be a very difficult work to carry out, was indeed based on a selfish desire.

It had become obvious that my dream of getting guidance from a guru from India was not going to fructify. If I was not disappointed and didn't feel a lack of anything it was because India and her people had shown me their greatness through their unbelievable capacity of tolerance. They accepted me completely. Left me to do whatever I wanted to do and to be wherever I wanted to be. They allowed me to shed my tears for reasons they may not have understood, and to laugh at my joys, whose cause may have escaped them. The greatness of the tolerance shown by India and the people of India was the channel for me to find peace with myself.

I wanted to give back something to India and the people of India, if possible, for being my guru.

Travelling through India was not the easiest task for a Korean in those days primarily due to the lack of a good Korean language guide book. I thought if I could write a useful travel guide book for Koreans, I could be useful to both my blood brothers and my spiritual brothers. When I realized this, writing the book became a compelling need.

In order to write my book, I spent a whole year travelling through India once again, this time with the aim of collecting information. Seeing India again with the eyes of a tourist and as a guide book writer and not as a spiritual seeker was an amazing experience in itself. It is not easy for me to say which part of me loved India more – the wandering sadhu or the tourist (or should I say, the seeker of history). Needless to say, the richness of the culture, heritage and traditions, in addition to the great beauty of the land, kept me enraptured through every single day of my stay in India.

When asked about marriage, Moojin used to reply that he wanted to get married to God. Gradually, as he reverted to the Buddhist faith of his early years, the specifics of the answer changed, but his attitude toward marriage remained sceptical.

But that, too, was to change. In the course of his second sojourn through India, he met Youn Sook, a Korean lady who was also travelling through India. Where Moojin was reserved and introverted, Youn Sook was loquacious and effervescent. While Moojin saw the misery and squalor of the human condition, Youn Sook enjoyed the ability of the human spirit to shine forth in the most trying conditions. They shared a love for India and a passion for liberation.

Moojin and Youn Sook started living together in 1996 and tied the knot in 2000.

Building a bridge between India and Korea became the mission of Moojin's life. 'These two cultures have ancient ties,' he said. In the first century CE, an Indian princess from Ayodhya is said to have travelled to Korea and married a Korean prince of a small principality called Gaya, possibly named after the Buddhist pilgrimage spot in India. The princess had a personality that was both endearing and strong. She won the hearts of her prince and his subjects and introduced many elements of Indian culture in Korea.

And so Moojin aimed to revive what had been lost with the passage of time. His book *We Are Now Going to India* was released in April 1996 by Minseo Publishing Co. and immediately became a bestseller. The number of tourists to India from Korea increased dramatically from that year. The book went into five reprints and sold 1.5 lakh copies. It was released in India in October 1996 by former Indian prime minister, Chandra Shekhar. Chandra Shekhar was apparently fascinated by the personality of the enigmatic Korean who seemed equally comfortable with prince and pauper alike, and till the end of his days received a supply of ginseng from Moojin.

The days of being a wandering sadhu were well and truly over. TV appearances, seminars and receptions became the order of the day. In August 1995, Youn Sook and Moojin had started a store called Passage to India in Seoul that sold Indian handicraft and travel packages. With the Korean economy doing well, the store started booming. Moojin began to be seen as the point man for all things related to India. He had good contacts in Delhi and he helped friends set up businesses. He connected Korean students wanting to study Buddhism with colleges in Pune that have excellent reputations for Buddhist studies. Fashion houses wanting to source textile and designs from India, real-estate companies wanting to buy properties in India, and politicians wanting to build ties with India started flocking to him. In between his business ventures, in a manner reminiscent of the great Russian painter Nicholas Roerich, Moojin found the time to lead expeditions lasting for several weeks into the heart of the Central Asian Himalayas.

This was the point at which Chang-Kwon began to use the *nom de plume* Moojin in his daily dealings. The word Moojin is a conjunction of 'moo' and 'jin'. Depending on the Chinese character used to write the name, 'moo' can mean nothingness, dance, force or duty; and 'jin' can mean truth, progress, dust or jewel. And these possible meanings are apparently just a start.

As expected, Moojin has a wonderful time explaining his name to people. Based on his mood, a range of meanings – the one who doesn't bother about (the so-called) truth, the one who has nothing more to progress toward, the one who is dancing in the world like dust, the one who has no jewel (money), the one whose force has no end, and the one who is nothing – can be ascribed to his name.

What I should call him had been a source of some light-hearted banter between us. When I first met him, he had told me I could call him Chang, which means 'creation', and was pronounced with an aspirated 'chh'. Perhaps inspired by movies in which East Asian names were prefixed by a mister, I began calling him Mr Chang. A few years into our association, he began objecting to the use of the prefix 'mister' as he felt it carried connotations of racist Westerners parodying the way East Asians referred to them – Mr Harry, Ms Mary, and so on. He wanted me to call him Chung (pronounced 'jeong' and connoting strength) or

Mr Chung, using the title only with the family name.

Even though I had lived in the United States and was used to people being sensitive about their names, I was rather bemused by Mr Chang's request. I had met and befriended a man with one name, and was unhappy to have to address him with some other combination of sounds. For me, it was almost as bad as someone asking me to change my feelings about a friend. My determination to hold my ground only hardened when Mr Chang started referring to me as 'Rohut'.

This little drama, entirely ridiculous in retrospect, ended only with the assumption of the *nom de plume* of Moojin. Among all the other reasons for rejoicing in the book that Mr Chang released, one was also that I could switch from Mr Chang to Moojin without having to give in on the request to move to Chung!

The Asian financial crisis hit South Korea hard by the middle of 1997 and caused a serious setback to Moojin's business. To make things worse, a travel partner in India, whom he had cultivated for years, disappeared overnight with all his business. Further worsening the situation, Youn Sook's health began to falter. She contracted diabetes and had to significantly cut down on her travel and business engagements. She had always been an invaluable ally to Moojin. She had the business instinct that he lacked and was the chief operating officer he needed.

Ironically, as Moojin's star was fading, other Koreans began to do well in the Indian market. Those he had helped set up shop started flourishing. Powerful Korean chaebols or multi-nationals – LG, Samsung, and many others – started looking at India as a viable market and ramping up operations here. Despite preparing the ground for ten years, Moojin was unable to catch the wave that made many Koreans operating in India multi-millionaires.

He set up a foundation called the Indo–Korean Foundation and started focussing on non-profit work. Operating on the premise that long-term business partnerships between countries could only be possible on a firm foundation of cultural affinity, he attempted to create partnerships between cities in India and South Korea.

Jaipur and Bangalore were his first targets. In Bangalore his efforts drew the attention of the uncrowned king of the city, Narayana Murthy, CEO of

Infosys, the bellwether of the Indian IT industry, who was deeply concerned about Bangalore's infrastructure bottlenecks and was eagerly looking for a partnership that could provide the city with a fresh lease of life. Moojin also tried to sign up with the cultural establishment in India to promote Indo–Korean art exhibitions and joint symposiums of Indian and Korean writers. He soon started hobnobbing with top bureaucrats, businessmen and artists in Delhi society.

But Moojin had not reckoned with the stasis of the Indian bureaucracy, its inertia in the face of all promising opportunity. Or, perhaps, he did not have the levers needed to move the bureaucrats. He found that his efforts generally failed, and even where they succeeded the credit went to the government officials on both sides rather than his foundation, which had done the legwork.

Other foundations with similar aims had been set up meanwhile, with better connections to industry and greater financial muscle. These foundations were able to navigate the Indian system more effectively.

And so, Moojin Chung, pioneer of the influx of Koreans to India, found himself excluded from the boom that happened in the first decade of the new millennium. He was given respect wherever he went and had access to the rich and the powerful in the Indo–Korean eco-system but had nothing much to show besides.

Now, Moojin has found a small niche helping the Indian embassy in South Korea to organize cultural extravaganzas that have taken the cultural wing of the embassy to an unprecedented level, but this is only a pale shadow of what might have been.

THE *final* SUTRA

'Moojin, I knew you as a spiritual seeker, a mystic, a philosopher, a lover of Indian culture, and an idealist, but I did not realize that you were also an entrepreneur.'

'Yes, I am an entrepreneur,' said Moojin turning his gaze fully upon mine. 'A failed entrepreneur.'

'But Moojin, you were so close to success so many times. With your book, your travel business, with your cultural mediation between India and South Korea. I would say you failed because you did not succeed, and it would have been as easy for you to have succeeded as it was for you to have failed.' The sad fate of my efforts at my business school seemed to pale in comparison to all he had gone through.

Moojin smiled. 'That is kind of you. But I cannot allow myself to think like that. I do not want to lose the fuel that spurs me on to my next ventures – the feeling I could have done better.'

'Why do you think you failed, Moojin?'

'I failed because of the lack of execution capability, because of a paucity of creative action. My team and I never had the ability to execute flawlessly on my vision. As a result, at crucial times, my projects fell through the cracks.'

Moojin saw that I was feeling despondent about what had befallen him.

'"Success closes as many opportunities as failure",' he laughed. 'You yourself would not have become a business professor and entrepreneur had you succeeded in your goal of becoming an eminent economic theorist in the United States. I would not have hobnobbed with the Delhi elite had my travel business taken off. Abhishek would probably not have taken the plunge with a start-up had he got into IIM Ahmedabad.

'If a project initiated by me does not fit into the universal scheme of things, despite my best intentions and efforts, who cares? The cosmos may have discarded my innovation for the time being, but who knows what will happen in the future?

'The game is never over. The universe has a pretty good knowledge management system and stores every new idea, every innovation ever attempted in its bottomless ledgers. When an idea will coalesce with some others to find expression in a more benign time can never be said. But it can, any time.'

'But you may not be around, then,' I said.

'Who cares?' he said slowly and with great emphasis. 'Running the cosmos is not my concern. The credit for making something work also does not belong to me. If one traces the network of causes, small and big, one will see that no attainment in this universe belongs to any one individual. A billion entities – little and large, seen and unseen, knowable and unknowable, visible and invisible, hidden and revealed, conspire to bring about the end result in a process that may, on occasion, have stretched for years. Behind any manifestation, therefore, is not an individual or a finite collective, but an emptiness. So I say, "who cares?"'

He went on, 'The seemingly successful are the fattened calves of nature and stand in very real danger of being led to the slaughterhouse through complacency, pride and smugness. But those who have fought honourably and valiantly and have failed are the salt of the earth, giving it fecundity, flavour, longevity.

'Those who do not allow failure to affect their morale realize that the human spirit can rise again from any adversity and create whatever it needs in the worst of circumstances. This realization is the basis of self-confidence. This self-confidence leads to detachment from possession and real freedom. The entrepreneur realizes that his or her real treasure is within, in the power to imagine, to come together with friends and to act. What need, then, of accumulation, of acquisitiveness? This is the last lesson that success needs to learn from failure in order to become abundance.'

'But, Moojin, I do not want to end up a mediocre person.'

I have never seen Moojin as fiery as he became when I made that remark.

'Do you think I am a mediocre person?' he demanded, his voice almost a shout.

'Do you think I am a mediocre person?' he repeated.

'Do you think there is any ordinary person? The most humdrum life hides depths, unseen struggles, unsung victories and unheard symphonies. The littlest birds, Professor, have the sweetest songs.

'One of the prices that many so-called successful people pay is losing sight of this fact. It is a heavy price indeed, as it prevents a true appreciation of the beauty of life. Using this attitude as a spur to greater achievement is good, but it has no truth in it in absolute terms, not even an iota.

'The mind loves to find causes of success and failure and identify winners and losers, but if we restrict ourselves to the life revealed to us through our ordinary faculties, we cannot hope to proceed very far in our understanding. The causes are often buried deep in the recesses of human minds, in worlds we cannot see, or histories we cannot access. This is why case studies analysing the success and failure of businesses, so much in vogue with business school professors, are so unsatisfactory. The writer force-fits the analysis with the benefit of hindsight.'

'Then what is the use of the qualities of entrepreneurship you elucidated?' I asked.

'Recipes for success are universal truths grounded in

the foundational principles of the universe. The wise can access these principles through introspection and intuition.'

I must say the conversation had meandered into planes that I had not expected. I was unsure if an entrepreneur needed to know all this. I also wanted to check if Moojin was hiding behind high-sounding philosophy to mask his failures.

'What next, Moojin?' I asked with the hint of a challenge in my voice.

'One million entrepreneurs,' he said slowly. 'My goal is to catalyse the birth of one million entrepreneurs. I am looking for corporate executives, plumbers, school-teachers, poets – in short, everyone. Maybe even business school professors and certainly, those most unsung entrepreneurs, the housewives. But it may not start as a mass movement. I want to mentor a handpicked group of people who can become catalysts of change.

'Socialism has failed, capitalism is faltering, communism is dead and Gandhi-ism has been taken hostage. It is only entrepreneurship that can yoke happiness and prosperity together for the vast majority of human beings.'

'And where do you intend to start?' I asked.

'With you,' he said, without the slightest trace of doubt. And for the umpteenth time that evening, I felt my smugness melt away.

Acknowledgements

In all innocence I had suggested to Thomas Abraham that he find an author to do an authentic book on entrepreneurship in India. Of course, I should have known that he would end up convincing me that I was the author he needed!

A big thank you to Moojin, Abhishek, Mekhla and Abhinav for sharing the stories of their remarkable lives with such candour and according me complete freedom in telling their tales.

To the legions of guinea pigs who sampled earlier versions of this 'moveable feast', my debt goes deeper than words. Foremost among my gentle critics – Taruni Mathur, Alok Agrawal, Rishi Prasad, K. Kaarthikeyan, Lalit Mathur, Geeta Mathur, Sajal Mathur, Arun Kumar, Ranjit Shastri, Kartikay Sahay, Ashesh Gupta, Gautam Kumar and Tanmay Gupta.

To the entrepreneurs whose stories of passion and courage gave me signposts to look out for – Taruna Ummat, Mayank Mansingh Kaul, Shiv Bhaskar Dravid – there will be a book on each of you some day!

To my network of marketing nodes who've generously given me access to their circle of friends – Geetika Sahay, Pranay Gupta, Prajakt Raut, Giridharee Saran, Siddharth Singh, Digbijoy Shukla, Arpit Agarwal, Sanjukt Saha, K. Srikrishna, Osama Manzar, P.K. Roy. As they said, 'A book is not a sack of potatoes.'

To my wise and generous editor, Poulomi Chatterjee, who knows when to push and when to leave well enough alone.

To my parents, who gave birth to the stories in me.

To Chaitanya and Soham, whose amazement that I was writing a book turned to disgust – 'You've *still* not finished!'

To Sonali, who said, 'I always knew you'd write a book.'